Salsa cooking

Salsa Cooking

Marjie Lambert

THE APPLE PRESS

DEDICATION

To my brothers, Ken and Robert, captive
audience to my earliest cooking experiments, and
my sisters-in-law, Nicky and Laveda, who now
have to put up with their eccentric tastes.

A QUINTET BOOK

Published by The Apple Press
6 Blundell Street
London N7 9BH

ISBN 1-85076-511-1

This book was designed and produced by
Quintet Publishing Limited
6 Blundell Street
London N7 9BH

Creative Director: Richard Dewing
Designer: Kerry Quested @ Design Revolution,
Brighton
Project Editor: Helen Denholm
Editor: Jane Middleton
Food Photographer: Andrew Sydenham
Home Economy: Nicola Fowler and Deborah
Greatrex

PICTURE CREDITS

Russell and Pamela Bamert: pages 11, 13, 25, 32,
39, 56, 110.
Travel Ink Photo & Feature Library: pages 45, 50.
Trip (© Richard Powers): page 29.
Peter Wilson: pages 2, 68, 81, 90, 96, 128.

ACKNOWLEDGEMENTS

With thanks to my friends George and Karen, to
Helen at Quintet, and as always to Terry.

Typeset in Great Britain by
Central Southern Typesetters, Eastbourne
Manufactured in Singapore by Eray Scan Pte Ltd
Printed in Singapore by Star Standard Pte Ltd

contents

INTRODUCTION

Most people think of salsa as a spicy tomato-onion-chilli sauce to eat with corn chips or tacos. However, there's much more to it than that. As the popularity of salsa has increased, it has come to mean sauces, relishes, and even chopped salads that almost always include some type of chilli but may not include tomatoes or onions. Instead, the main ingredient may be fruit, black beans, sweetcorn, or even unexpected vegetables like radishes or courgettes.

The definition of salsa has to be elastic. As soon as you find a rule, you find the exception. Not every salsa contains chillies. Typically salsa is used as a condiment, but some, such as Black Bean-Sweetcorn Salsa, are so hearty that they need no accompaniment. Salsas may be raw or cooked, but often in an uncooked salsa some of the ingredients are grilled or barbecued to add flavour or mellow a raw taste.

Salsas go with all kinds of food. In addition to corn chips, they are marvellous with grilled meats and seafood, on eggs, over pasta, in salad, stirred into steamed vegetables and, of course, over Mexican dishes like tacos and chillies rellenos. Some salsas are even served with ice cream.

The word salsa is Spanish for sauce, and salsas have their roots in Mexico. However, they have long been a fixture in the Caribbean, South and Central America, and the south-western United States, too. In the 1990s, the passion for salsa has spread into other parts of the United States and Europe. In 1992, North Americans spent twice as much on salsas and other Mexican sauces as they did on ketchup, formerly their favourite condiment, and sales of salsa are still growing.

An ever-increasing number of brands of salsa are available in the shops. They are not only the bottled varieties that have been stocked for years in the foreign-food sections of supermarkets and grocers, but also fresh, uncooked salsas available in the chill cabinets. In the bottling process, salsas are heated to nearly 93°C/200°F, eliminating their fresh taste and much of their texture.

While bottled salsas still dominate the market, a growing share is being taken over by speciality and gourmet salsas at the expense of the major brands that have been around for years – evidence that people are looking for more adventurous tastes in their salsas. Salsa ingredients, especially a growing range of fresh and dried chillies, are also gaining shelf space.

It is not difficult to see why salsa has become so popular. People are fascinated by ethnic foods, particularly spicy ones, and tastes from different cuisines become mixed in exciting, new combinations. Convenience is a priority, and most salsas are easy to make. Salsa meets the current demand for healthy foods. Made of fresh fruit or vegetables, chillies, herbs, and just a dash of olive oil, salsa is often a healthy alternative to traditional sauces with fat and cream.

Paul Prudhomme, the gregarious promoter of Cajun food, likes to talk about food creating a "round" sensation in the mouth, with different flavours setting off different tastebuds, until the whole palate is dancing. A good, fresh salsa has much the same effect. It is a marvellous mix of flavours, some subtle, some aggressive, accompanied by the kick of hot chillies.

In this book, you will find more than 40 salsa recipes. They range from variations on the basic tomato-onion-chilli mix, to black bean salsas, sweetcorn salsas, fruit salsas, and salsas based on roasted chillies. There are raw salsas and cooked salsas; winter salsas, for when tomatoes and chillies are out of season, and even dessert salsas for spooning over ice cream. Hopefully, you will find inspiration for your own creations, using these recipes as a basis.

There are also plenty of ideas on how to use the salsas, with recipes for appetizers, soups, salads, side dishes, main courses and desserts. While the list of salsa recipes is meant to be comprehensive, the range of other recipes in this book is not. Instead, they are intended to be a sampling of what is possible, a starting point for your own imagination.

INGREDIENTS

CHILLIES

Chillies are grown all around the world – consider the sweet pimento that produces Hungary's famous paprika, the hot red Thai chilli, and the incendiary Scotch bonnet of the Caribbean. However, Mexico is king when it comes to chillies, with about 100 varieties, only a few of which are commonly available outside Mexico.

Buying chillies can be a very frustrating experience because they are frequently mislabelled or not labelled at all. Many supermarkets stock several varieties of fresh chillies and tell you only what you can see for yourself, that they are red or green. You are left to guess whether they are Anaheims or serranos, habaneros or poblanos, and even how hot they are. Dried chillies are often mislabelled by the packager, in part because the same chilli will have different names in different parts of Mexico. It is a good idea to learn to identify your favourite varieties on sight.

All chillies belong to the *Capsicum* family. Their heat comes from capsaicin, a compound that is concentrated not in the seeds, as is commonly believed, but in the white fleshy placenta and veins, particularly around the stem. Cut open a jalapeño chilli and you will probably see thin streaks of orange running through the veins – that is capsaicin. You can adjust the level of heat in a recipe by removing all the veins and seeds for a milder dish or leaving them for a hotter dish.

In 1902 Wilbur Scoville, a pharmacologist, searched for a way to rank the relative heat of chillies. He mixed ground chillies with sugar, alcohol and water, then graded them according to how much the substance had to be diluted before no heat was detectable. Now the same ranking is done by computerized technology; zero for sweet peppers, 10,000 for jalapeños, 35,000 for serranos, and 150,000 to 200,000 for habaneros and Scotch bonnet chillies.

FRESH CHILLIES

The chillies below are listed according to their strength, from the mildest to the hottest. However, it is difficult to give an exact guide, since the same type of chilli can vary widely in heat, depending on the growing conditions.

Anaheim Also known as the California chilli, this is pale green, about 15 cm/6 in long, skinny, and relatively flat. Mild in flavour, it is good roasted and peeled, and is often stuffed and used in chillies rellenos.

New Mexico The New Mexico chilli resembles the Anaheim, although it is a little hotter. Green New Mexico chillies are available for only a short time each autumn outside New Mexico. Most are allowed to ripen to a bright red and are then dried. They are available in their dried form, and are the type used in *ristras,* hanging bunches of dried chillies.

Poblano These green-black chillies have broad shoulders, narrowing to the tip, and resemble dark, emaciated sweet peppers. Moderately spicy, they are never eaten raw, but are roasted and peeled. They are often used in chillies rellenos. Poblanos are often incorrectly called pasillas, both in their fresh and dried state.

7

SUBSTITUTING CHILLIES

Although markets carry more varieties of chillies than they did just a few years ago, it isn't always possible to find a particular chilli specified in a recipe. Feel free to substitute one chilli for another, keeping in mind any difference in their heat. Remember that the salsa's heat is affected as much by how closely you trim the seeds and veins as by the type of chilli you use.

Some tips for substituting chillies:

▶ Sweet red or green peppers contain none of the substance that causes chillies to be hot, and should not be used as a substitute for chillies.

▶ Unless you're trying to increase or decrease the spiciness of the salsa, try to find another chilli that has approximately the same degree of heat as the one called for in the recipe. While a serrano chilli is an excellent substitute for a jalapeño, an Anaheim is not. No matter how many Anaheims you put in the salsa, it will not be as hot as a jalapeño salsa.

▶ Some of the larger chillies with tougher skins, such as poblanos and Anaheims, are usually roasted and peeled before they are added to salsa. Although substituting roast chillies for raw – or vice versa – will change the character of the salsa, the flavour will still be good.

▶ If all you can find are dried chillies, choose a cooked salsa recipe. It is difficult to make a good uncooked salsa with reconstituted dried chillies.

Jalapeño These glossy green chillies are probably the most widely used variety outside Mexico. They are smooth-skinned, narrow, and about 7.5 cm/3 in long. Although they are hot, their heat is much reduced if they are seeded and veined. They can be used raw, roasted, pickled, smoked, or dried. If left to ripen, they turn red.

8

Serrano Slightly hotter than jalapeños, these are small, about 5 cm/2 in long and very skinny. They are ripe when dark green, but if left on the plant will continue ripening to a bright red. They are most often eaten raw in salsas.

Habanero These chillies of the Yucatan, along with the related Scotch bonnet of the Caribbean, are just about the hottest chillies in creation. The habanero is only very

occasionally available, but is commonly used as an ingredient in bottled hot sauces. It looks like a miniature sweet pepper or lantern, perhaps 5 cm/2 in long, and its colour can range from green to orange-red.

Other fresh chillies occasionally available in markets specializing in imported foods are the **cayenne,** long, skinny, bright red and hot, most commonly dried and ground into cayenne pepper; the **cubanelle,** a long and skinny yellow or pale green chilli – mild and sweet, it can be substituted for Anaheim chillies; the **pasilla,** also known as chilli negro, a slim purple-black chilli that is moderately spicy, like the poblano; the **fresno,** sometimes called wax chilli or chilli caribe, a very hot chilli that is similar in size to the jalapeño but a bit more triangular, and ranges from pale green to bright red. Fresno chillies are also sometimes called **chilli gueros,** which is actually a generic name for pale green or yellow chillies.

DRIED CHILLIES
California These are dried Anaheims, mild, long, skinny and red-brown.

Ancho This is the dried version of the poblano. It has a very pleasant spiciness that is hot but still easily tolerable. The ancho is often mislabelled pasilla, but is distinguishable when held up to the light by its red-brown colour; in the same light, a true pasilla is brown-black.

New Mexico The New Mexico chilli, cousin to the Anaheim, is allowed to ripen until it is red and hot. It is widely available in dried form.

Cascabel Cascabel refers to both the fresh and dried form of this round, dark red-brown chilli, but it is most often available dried. Medium hot and slightly fruity, it is good lightly toasted, then crumbled and added to sauces.

Chipotle This is the jalapeño chilli, smoked and dried. It is hot, and adds a wonderful, smoky flavour to salsas and cooked dishes. It is also available canned in adobo sauce or pickled. Once you become familiar with the chipotle, you'll want to add it to everything!

Chilli de Arbol This short, skinny, red-orange chilli is very hot. It is usually a dried red serrano, but may also be one of the other small hot peppers such as cayenne or Thai. Unhelpful packagers may even label chilli de Arbol simply as "red chillies".

MISCELLANEOUS
Chilli flakes, or dried crushed chillies
Sometimes sold as chillies caribe, these are usually dried, crushed New Mexico red chillies, and are hot. They are the chilli flakes often seen in pizzerias.

Chilli powder Chilli powder is a commercial seasoning mix that includes ground chillies and other spices. It is only mildly to moderately spicy. Pure ground dried chilli powder is more typically available from specialist suppliers than in the spice section of a supermarket. It is usually hotter than chilli powder, but how hot depends on the type of chilli. Most common are California chilli powder, consisting of dried ground Anaheims, and a hotter powder usually made with chimayo chillies from New Mexico. Cayenne and paprika are also dried, ground chillies.

Canned chillies Except for chipotle chillies, canned chillies are not recommended, since they lose much of their taste and texture in processing.

TOMATOES

If chillies are the diva of salsa, tomatoes are the chorus. When they're good, they provide a solid – and often unnoticed – background for the star. But when they're bad, they mar the entire performance. Try to avoid pre-packed supermarket tomatoes, the hard, pink, flavourless kind. Some shops now stock organically grown (as opposed to chemically ripened) tomatoes, usually at a higher price. Buy the riper ones. Alternatively, buy small Italian tomatoes that are meatier and travel better than larger tomatoes, so they may be riper. You can also use canned whole tomatoes, or grill the hard tomatoes, a process that adds flavour even to the worst pre-packed tomatoes. Best of all, grow your own or buy just-picked tomatoes from a country farm shop.

ONIONS

Onions are a crucial ingredient in most salsas. They are good both raw and roasted. Use white or yellow onions unless the recipe specifies otherwise. Red onions are also excellent in salsas, although the flat Spanish reds do not hold up well in cooking. Spring or green onions add a sharp flavour and a crunch to uncooked salsas. Mild sweet onions are becoming more widely available from greengrocers selling a wide range of vegetables and can add a different twist.

TOMATILLOS

Because of their appearance, tomatillos are sometimes called green tomatoes, or little tomatoes, and they are often used in place of tomatoes in salsa. In fact they are members of the gooseberry family. They have a papery outer husk that must be removed, and they should be rinsed to get rid of the sticky residue on the surface of the husked tomatillo. Peek under the husk to see how ripe they are. Bright green tomatillos are not ripe; look for pale green to yellowish ones. If you use unripe tomatillos, the salsa will be tart. You can add a little sugar to offset the tartness.

GARLIC

Garlic is a staple ingredient in many salsas. Use fresh minced garlic, never garlic powder or salt. Bottled minced garlic is acceptable. Roasting or baking garlic mellows its sharp taste and gives salsas a good flavour.

AVOCADOS

There are two commonly available types of avocados. The most flavourful is the Haas, which has black, bumpy skin and is plentiful in late spring until early autumn. The Fuerte has a greener, smoother skin and is not as flavourful, but is available during the winter. Avocados can be temperamental, seemingly going from hard and flavourless to mushy and bad-tasting in little more than a day. The best way to use avocados is to buy them a few days in advance of when you want to use them, while they are still hard, then let them ripen on a kitchen work surface, away from direct sunlight. They will ripen slightly faster if you close them in a paper bag with an apple. Do not refrigerate them before they are ripe. Once they are ripe, they will keep for a day or two in the refrigerator. In an emergency, add a little avocado oil to improve the flavour of a mashed, not-quite-ripe avocado.

9

SWEET PEPPERS AND SWEET CHILLIES

Although they are related to chillies, sweet peppers do not contain any capsaicin and cannot be substituted for chillies. Green peppers are only occasionally added to salsa. The sweet red pepper – which is simply a ripe green pepper – is more frequently used, either raw or roasted. Because of its sweetness, the raw red pepper marries well with fruit salsas and adds crunch. Roasted and peeled, it is a delicious savoury addition to many salsas. Other sweet or mild chillies, such as the Italian sweet chilli or the Hungarian pimento, can be added to salsa for texture and flavour, although they are not a substitute for spicy chillies. Remove veins and seeds before using.

10

FRUITS

Fruit salsas are more popular in the Caribbean and the United States than in Mexico. They are excellent with broiled meats and seafood. Tropical fruits, especially mango, papaya and pineapple, are surprisingly good when combined with hot chillies, and are often grilled for a sweet smoky flavour. Grilled pineapple is particularly good. *Mangoes* should be firm but not hard – slightly less ripe for salsas than for eating plain – and yellow to red-orange (although some new varieties of mango are ripe when green). If not picked too green, they can be ripened on a kitchen work surface. *Papayas* should be yellow with no more than a few green streaks, and no soft spots; they will ripen a little at home. *Pineapple* should be more gold than green, with no soft spots, and should have a sweet

perfume. They do not ripen after they are picked. *Peaches* and *nectarines* should be slightly soft. They will ripen on a kitchen work surface or in a paper bag if they were not picked too green.

JICAMA

This Mexican tuber with crisp white flesh and a thin brown skin should be peeled and eaten raw. It has a very mild flavour and is valued mostly for the crunch it adds to salsas and salads. In Mexico, slices of raw jicama are drizzled with lime juice and sprinkled with chilli powder, then eaten as a snack.

BEANS

Beans are a staple ingredient of the Latin American diet, so it is not surprising that they are a popular ingredient in, or partner to, salsa. Black beans, also sometimes known as turtle beans, are the usual type in salsas. They have a smoky, nutty flavour, but need salt and other herbs or spices to complement it.

CHORIZO

Chorizo is a spicy Mexican sausage, most often made with pork but sometimes with beef. Paprika is usually the predominant spice, but the ingredients may vary widely, and the seasonings in a dish containing chorizo should

be adjusted accordingly. The fat content also varies. Chorizo adds excellent flavour to beans and eggs.

HERBS AND SPICES

CORIANDER

The most popular herb or spice used in salsa is coriander, a pungent member of the parsley family. Also known as cilantro or Chinese parsley, fresh coriander is available in most supermarkets. Dried coriander is almost never used in salsa, and coriander seeds are not a substitute for fresh coriander. Look for coriander with bright green leaves, and with roots attached. Pick off yellow leaves and store in a plastic bag in the refrigerator, with roots, but not the leaves, wrapped in a wet paper towel.

CUMIN

Cumin seed, native to the Mediterranean, is a staple ingredient in Mexican cooking. In the United Kingdom it is more frequently sold in its ground form, although some cooks like to toast and grind the seeds themselves. It is excellent with beans, and is occasionally used in salsas. Use it sparingly.

OREGANO

Choose Mexican oregano, which has a stronger flavour than the Greek, and use it in dried-leaf form, not ground. Some cooks like to toast oregano briefly in an ungreased frying pan before using. Be careful not to scorch it. Other herbs occasionally used in salsa are *basil,* which marries well with tomatoes although it is not a traditional salsa ingredient; fresh *mint,* which also goes well with tomatoes, and with some fruit salsas; fresh *ginger,* seen more often in Caribbean salsas; and *epazote,* a medicinally flavoured weed also known as wormseed or Mexican tea, which is hard to find in the United Kingdom, but is popular in southern Mexico in salsas and bean dishes.

COOKING TECHNIQUES

Once making salsa was easy: you simply chopped tomatoes, onions, chillies, and perhaps some coriander or another herb, added a squeeze of lime juice and a pinch of salt, and you had salsa. But now that salsa has become so popular, there are all sorts of variations on the basic theme, such as roasting ingredients to give a good, rich flavour, or cooking salsa for a more concentrated sauce. Food processors have made a difference too, but if they are not used with care they can turn what should be a rough-textured mix of distinct ingredients into a mushy soup. The chunky textures are part of a salsa's charm. Below are some pointers for successful salsa making.

Strings of chillies for sale at the Hatch Chile Festival in New Mexico.

PROTECTING YOUR SKIN

The capsaicin in chillies can burn your skin, and what's worse, if you get it on your hands you're likely to get it in your eyes, too. You don't realize how often you rub your eyes and touch the tender skin on your face until you do it with capsaicin on your hands. It's particularly painful if you get it in your contact lenses. Never touch your lenses if you have been handling chillies; your eyes are far more sensitive than your hands, and a little tingle on your fingertip will turn into sharp pain in your eye. The solution is to wear rubber gloves when working with chillies. Even a plastic sandwich bag will do. In moments of desperation, use a piece of cling film to protect your hand.

If you do get capsaicin on your hands, running plain water over them won't help, since capsaicin is not water-soluble. At worst, water will spread the pain. Soap up the spot, then rinse. Sometimes it helps to massage vegetable fat into the skin, then wash it off with soap and water.

ROASTING AND GRILLING

Roasting adds flavour to salsa ingredients. Even hard, insipid pre-packed tomatoes are improved by roasting over an open flame. The process also blisters chilli and pepper skins and makes them easy to remove. Another advantage of roasting is that it cooks out much of the excess juice from tomatoes, so that you don't end up with a pool of watery tomato juice in your salsa.

Traditional Mexican roasting involves using a comal, or Mexican griddle. Cast-iron frying pans are, however, an acceptable substitute. Roasting over an open flame is the preferred method, but cooking under a grill is also effective, although of course it doesn't add the delicious smoky flavour.

Chillies and peppers can be roasted whole or cut into large, flat sections. Turn the skin side toward the heat source, and check them frequently. The skin will blister slightly and develop some brown spots, and gradually become charred and completely blistered. Chillies with uneven surfaces, like poblanos, will not cook as evenly as a straight-sided red sweet pepper, but that's all right. Be careful that the heat chars only the skin, not the flesh, and do not turn the fleshy side towards the heat. If you are roasting whole chillies, turn until all sides are done.

Remove the chillies or peppers from the heat when the skin is completely blistered and mostly browned or blackened. This can take just 2 or 3 minutes a side over flaming coals, or 10 minutes or longer under a grill. Put the chillies or peppers in a plastic bag or a covered bowl and let them steam for about 10 minutes, then scrape or pull off the skin. It should come away easily, but it's fine if some bits of blackened skin remain; they will add to the flavour. Remember that cooking does not neutralize the capsaicin, so you still need to protect your skin. If you cooked the chillies or peppers whole, remove the seeds.

If you only need to roast one or two chillies, you can do so over the flame of a gas burner. Pinch the chilli in long tongs or impale it on the end of a long fork, and hold it at the top of the flame. This process is as effective as the others, but it is time-consuming since you can do only one at a time.

Dried chillies gain a tasty flavour from roasting. Put them in a 120°C/250°F/Gas Mark ½ oven for 5 minutes or so, or in an ungreased frying pan, until they darken slightly and turn brittle. Do not allow them to blacken or they will taste bitter. Once roasted, they will crumble easily.

Roasting adds flavour to *tomatoes,* too, especially if it is done over an open flame. Cut the tomatoes in half horizontally and squeeze out most of the seeds and excess juice. Place with the skin side towards the heat, and cook

1. Barbecue or grill the chillies or peppers until the skin is mostly blackened.

2. Remove from the heat and place in a plastic bag or a covered bowl for about 10 minutes.

3. Scrape or pull off the skin. You can leave a few of the blackened bits for extra flavour.

until the skin is partly blackened and slips off easily. If you're cooking over an open flame, turn the cut side towards the flame and cook briefly. To cook tomatoes under a grill, place them cut-side down on a flameproof baking sheet. If the baking sheet does not have edges, line it with foil and crimp the foil to create a shallow basin to catch the juice. When the tomatoes are done, slip off their skins and let the tomatoes cool in a colander so that excess liquid drains off.

Follow the same steps to roast thick slices of onion, unpeeled garlic cloves, husked tomatillos, or wedges of mango or pineapple. *Onions* should be roasted on both sides until softened, partially browned and fragrant. *Garlic cloves* should be watched carefully as they are easily scorched and will turn bitter. They should soften slightly. *Tomatillos* will turn soft, lose their shape and brown slightly. *Pineapple and mango slices* should brown slightly. Remember, you are adding flavour, not thoroughly cooking these ingredients.

RECONSTITUTING DRIED CHILLIES

Slit open the chilli and remove the stem and however many seeds you want. With dried chipotles the stems can be more easily removed after soaking. The chillies will reconstitute quicker if you cut the two sides apart and separate them into two pieces. Put the dried chillies in a small, heat-resistant bowl, pour boiling water over them, and let them steep until they are pliable. Warning: Some of the capsaicin will rise in the steam and can briefly irritate your nose, throat and lungs. Try not to breathe in the steam. The water will leach some of the flavour out of dried chillies, so use as little water as possible, and leave them to soak for as short a time as necessary, usually 20 to 30 minutes. If the chillies are very dry and brittle, you can simmer them in water on the hob instead of soaking.

12

Process the chillies with their soaking water, fresh water or stock, as directed in the recipe. Strain to remove the bits of skin, if you wish. A good guideline is to strain the chillies if you are making a smooth sauce, but not to bother if they are going into a chunky salsa.

CHOPPING AND PROCESSING

The best uncooked salsa is made by hand, using a sharp knife. It is amazing how much faster and easier chopping is when your knives are well sharpened. Dull knives can bruise food, make cooking tedious, increase your chances of getting burnt by the capsaicin in chillies, and prompt you to throw everything in the food processor. It is very tempting to do this anyway. A food processor chops and mixes everything in a few seconds, and you are less likely to burn your hands with capsaicin. It can also turn your salsa into a

mushy blend that has lost the individual flavours of its ingredients. For this reason, it is best to use the food processor sparingly and carefully. So here are some rules to follow to help you if you really must use the food processor – such as when guests are expected in five minutes and you still haven't made the salsa.

1. Chop at least some of the ingredients by hand so that the salsa will have some texture. The food processor is best used for sturdier ingredients such as onions, garlic and roast chillies. Ingredients such as tomatoes and raw chillies have a higher proportion of water, and turn into a watery mess in the processor. Chop at least one tomato, and preferably all, by hand.

2. Use the processor's pulse button. It is better to process food in short bursts and check its consistency after each burst than to run it steadily until you have soup.

3. Add tomatoes after hardier items like onions are partially chopped. It takes longer to chop an onion in the food processor than it does to ruin tomatoes.

The rules change when you are making a cooked salsa and are looking for a smoother texture. Also, cooking will cause much of the watery liquid to evaporate. Again, however, you should use the processor sparingly, processing the salsa in short bursts rather than running it steadily.

The food processor is a useful tool when the primary ingredient in the salsa is roasted chillies or peppers. The roasting dries some of the water from the flesh and makes it sturdier. However, roast chillies can be a bit stringy, leaving you with long threads, even after processing. Cut roast chillies into strips across their width before putting them in the processor. This quick step avoids stringiness.

13

Serving spicy salsas at a chilli festival in New Mexico. Wearing protective gloves like these helps to avoid the capsaicin in the chillies from burning your hands.

USEFUL TIPS

▶ If you are cooking salsa to reduce the liquid, use a wide, shallow pan rather than a deep saucepan. The liquid will boil off more quickly without overcooking the salsa.

▶ Allow uncooked salsas to stand for at least 30 minutes while the flavours meld, then taste and adjust the seasonings.

▶ To peel tomatoes, put them in a pan of boiling water for 30 to 40 seconds. The skins will slip off easily.

▶ Don't use aluminium pans or bowls. The acid in salsas will react with the metal and give the salsa a metallic taste.

uncooked salsas

Roast Jalapeño Salsa
Guacamole
Salsa Cruda I
Salsa Cruda II
Salsa Cruda III
Sweet Red Pepper Salsa
Cucumber Salsa
Sweetcorn Salsa
Courgette Salsa

Avocado Salsa
Olive Salsa
Tomato-Mint Salsa
Tomatillo-Habanero Salsa
Spicy Herb Salsa
Cactus Salsa
Barbecued Salsa
Black Bean Salsa
Coriander-Chilli Pesto
Kitchen Sink Guacamole
Radish Salsa
Roast Sweetcorn Salsa

Roast Jalapeño Salsa

Makes about 250 g/9 oz

At first glance, this salsa may seem unbearably hot. But when the jalapeños are trimmed of seeds and veins, then roasted, they take on a wonderful mellow flavour that is only moderately spicy. Try this salsa on biscuits, over steamed vegetables, or on meat or fish.

Ingredients

15 jalapeño chillies
4 Anaheim chillies
3 × 1-cm/½-in thick slices of red onion, peeled
5 cloves garlic, unpeeled
¼ tsp dried oregano
2 tbsp olive oil
1 tbsp fresh lemon juice
¼ tsp salt

16

Method

► Cut the jalapeños and Anaheims in half, and remove the seeds and veins. Cook the chillies, onion slices and garlic over a barbecue kettle, or under a grill, remembering to keep the skins of the chillies facing the heat source. The chillies will cook unevenly, and it's not necessary for the skins to be completely blackened. Don't cook them until they are charred through to the flesh. Remove them from the heat when they are ready and seal in a plastic bag or foil pouch. Leave them in the bag or pouch for 10 minutes. This will loosen the skins and make them easier to remove.

► The onion slices should soften and brown slightly. Turn and cook them on both sides. Turn the garlic once and cook until cloves are softened. Garlic will turn bitter if it is charred, so watch it closely.

► With a sharp knife, peel and scrape the skins off the chillies. Jalapeño skins are not as tough as many other chillies, so it's all right to leave part of the skin on. Roast chillies have a tendency to get stringy, so cut them in strips from side to side, not lengthwise. Put the strips in a food processor.

► Cut each onion slice into quarters and add them to the food processor. Peel the garlic, trim off any burnt spots, and add that too. Add remaining ingredients and process until they are well chopped but not a paste. The mixture will be fairly dry.

Guacamole

In its most primitive form, guacamole is nothing but mashed avocados and tomatoes. Most guaçamoles and avocado salsas are a little more complex than that, but the best are made from a minimum of ingredients – avocados, onions, chillies, lime juice, salt and pepper.

That doesn't mean that a guacamole made with exotic ingredients is no good. Avocados go well with blue cheese, anchovies, and any number of other unorthodox additions. To prove it, there is a recipe for Kitchen Sink Guacamole on page 28, made with bacon and olives. Just don't let the wonderful flavour of a perfectly ripe avocado be overwhelmed by unnecessary ingredients.

Some tips for making guacamole and avocado salsas:

► Guacamole is supposed to be lumpy. Don't purée the avocados. Mash them with a fork, or use a hand mixer, but only briefly.

► Don't add the avocados until just before serving, or they will turn an unappetizing brown. That can be delayed by mixing the avocado chunks with lime juice, but not for long. Contrary to popular belief, putting an avocado stone in the guacamole will not keep it from turning brown.

► Buy hard avocados a few days before you plan to make guacamole, and let them ripen in a paper bag or on a kitchen work surface, away from direct sunlight. If their flavour is still a little short of perfection, mix in a few drops of avocado oil.

Guacamole

Makes about 450 g/1 lb

This guacamole is made for corn chips, but it's also good on meat or taco salads. There is a little kick in the aftertaste from the hot pepper sauce, but it won't be very spicy unless you add some of the jalapeño seeds. I like my guacamole chunky, so I use a hand mixer rather than a food processor to blend the ingredients, then add some diced avocado afterwards for texture. You can prepare the other ingredients in advance, but don't add the avocado until just before serving.

INGREDIENTS

2 avocados, peeled, stoned and diced
2 tomatoes, grilled, skinned and chopped
2 tbsp finely minced onion
2 cloves garlic, minced
2 jalapeño chillies, minced
1 tbsp olive oil
1 tbsp fresh lemon juice
dash of hot pepper sauce
salt and pepper to taste

METHOD

▶ Core the tomatoes, cut them in half and squeeze the seeds out. Place the tomatoes cut side down on a flameproof baking sheet and place them under the grill. (*Note:* If the baking sheet does not have sides, line it with foil, then crimp the edges to form a shallow basin to catch the tomato juice.) Grill the tomatoes until the skin is just slightly blackened and loose. Slide off their skins, drain off excess juices, and let them cool.

▶ Using a hand mixer, combine about three-quarters of the diced avocado with all the remaining ingredients except salt and pepper. It should be slightly lumpy. Mix in the remaining avocado chunks, and add salt and pepper to taste. Serve immediately.

Clockwise from the top: *Salsa Cruda I (page 18), Guacamole and Roast Jalapeño Salsa.*

17

How Hot Is It?

How hot are these salsas? The answer is, as hot as you want them to be. The heat of a salsa depends not so much on how many chillies it contains, but on how they are cleaned and trimmed.

The heat of a chilli comes from capsaicin, which is concentrated in the veins. Because the seeds are in contact with the veins, they taste hot too. If you trim all the seeds and veins from a chilli it will be surprisingly mild.

Try this experiment: make two batches of any of the Salsa Cruda recipes. In one batch, trim away all the seeds and veins from the chillies. In the other, toss all the seeds and veins into the salsa. Now taste the difference.

After you have experimented with the seeds and veins, and know your preference, you can adjust all the salsa recipes in this book to your own preferred level of heat.

But what can you do when a salsa is too hot?

▶ Olive oil and puréed tomato can both help lower the heat of salsa by small degrees.

▶ If a salsa is much too hot, make a second batch, omitting the chillies, then combine the two batches.

▶ Dairy products such as soured cream can be mixed with salsa to combat the heat. The resulting salsa will have an entirely different character, but it will be far more tolerable.

18

Salsa Cruda I

Makes about 250 g/9 oz

This is a basic tomato salsa, made with barbecued or grilled tomatoes (see picture on page 17), and is good for dipping corn chips or spooning over egg dishes or tostadas.

It is pleasantly spicy rather than hot, but can be made more piquant if you don't trim away the jalapeño veins and seeds. It can be made several hours in advance.

Ingredients

3 large tomatoes, cored and halved
75 g/3 oz finely chopped onion
2 cloves garlic, minced
2 jalapeño chillies, seeded and minced
3 tbsp finely chopped coriander
1 tbsp olive oil
1 tbsp fresh lime juice
salt to taste

Method

▶ Core the tomatoes, cut them in half and squeeze the seeds out. Place the tomatoes cut side down on a flameproof baking sheet and place them under the grill. (*Note:* If the baking sheet does not have sides, line it with foil, then crimp the edges to form a shallow basin to catch the tomato juice.) Grill the tomatoes until the skin is just slightly blackened and loose. Slide off their skins, drain off excess juices, and let them cool.

▶ While the tomatoes are cooling, mix together all the remaining ingredients. Then chop the tomatoes and add them to the salsa. Let stand for 15 minutes or so, then taste and adjust the seasoning.

Salsa Cruda II

Makes about 200 g/7 oz

This salsa has a lower proportion of tomatoes than the other two, and uses the hotter serrano chillies. It is an all-purpose salsa, good with corn chips, over tacos and tostadas, with meat and fish, or mixed into rice.

Ingredients

4 medium tomatoes, cored and halved
175 g/6 oz chopped onion
5 serrano chillies, partly seeded if desired, minced
2 cloves garlic, minced
3 tbsp chopped fresh coriander
2 tbsp fresh lime juice
1 tbsp olive oil
¼ to ½ tsp salt

Method

▶ Cut the tomatoes in half and squeeze out seeds. Grill the tomatoes cut side down on a flameproof baking sheet until skins are partly blackened and skins slip off easily. Remove from heat. Let them cool in a colander so excess liquids drain off and then remove the skins. Purée in a blender or food processor, but do not purée so long that the tomato becomes liquefied.

▶ Stir all the remaining ingredients together and add the tomatoes. Let stand for 30 minutes, then taste and adjust the seasoning.

Salsa Cruda III

Clockwise from the top: Salsa Cruda III, Cucumber Salsa (page 20) and Sweet Red Pepper Salsa (page 20).

Makes about 575 g/1¼ lb salsa

The tomatoes are not grilled in this recipe, so the salsa is more chunky than soupy. It is good with corn chips, and can also be used as a topping for eggs, tostadas and soups, or mixed into vegetables. It is medium hot but can be made hotter by leaving in the jalapeño seeds.

INGREDIENTS

4 large tomatoes, seeded and chopped
75 g/3 oz chopped sweet pepper
50 g/2 oz chopped red onion
40 g/1½ oz chopped spring onion
3 jalapeño chillies, seeded and chopped
3 tbsp chopped fresh coriander
2 cloves garlic, minced
1 tbsp fresh lime juice
salt and pepper to taste

METHOD

▶ Combine all the ingredients. Let stand for about 15 minutes, then taste and adjust the salt and pepper. For a more liquid salsa, increase the amount of lime juice and/or add a little olive oil or other vegetable oil.

Sweet Red Pepper Salsa

Makes about 250 g/9 oz

Roasted red sweet peppers are the main ingredient in this versatile salsa (see picture on page 19), which has an unexpectedly sweet flavour. It is excellent with meat or fish, in an omelette, over pasta or steamed vegetables, or as a spread for biscuits. For colour, substitute yellow, orange or purple sweet peppers for some of the red.

INGREDIENTS

4 sweet red peppers
2 1-cm/½-in thick slices onion, peeled
3 cloves garlic, unpeeled
2 serrano chillies, chopped and partly seeded
2 tbsp olive oil
1 tbsp chopped fresh basil or 1 tsp dried
1 tsp grated lemon rind
2 tbsp red wine vinegar
¼ tsp salt

METHOD

▶ To roast the red peppers, cut them into 4 or 5 pieces lengthwise so that they will lie relatively flat. Place the red peppers, onion slices and unpeeled garlic on a barbecue or under the grill. The garlic should soften slightly, but needs to be watched closely as it scorches easily and turns bitter. The onions should be turned once, and should be softened and slightly browned. The skin of the red peppers should always face the heat source, and should be blistered and blackened, but take care not to char them so completely that the flesh is burnt.

▶ Remove the peppers from the fire or the grill as they blacken. They will probably cook unevenly. As you remove them, place them in a bag, a foil pouch, or a covered bowl. The steamy heat will loosen the skin and make it easy to remove after about 10 minutes.

▶ Pull the skin off the peppers. Because they have a tendency to get stringy lengthwise, cut them into several strips across their width. Peel the garlic cloves and trim off any scorched spots. Cut each onion slice into quarters. Put the peppers, onions, and garlic into a blender or food processor with the remaining ingredients. Process until the ingredients are well chopped but not so finely chopped that the salsa turns into a paste. Taste and adjust the seasoning.

Cucumber Salsa

Makes about 450 g/1 lb

Radishes and cucumbers make this a crunchy salsa, good for topping soups and pozole (page 81), or as a dressing in a pitta bread sandwich. With three jalapeños, it is moderately hot. See picture on page 19.

INGREDIENTS

1 small or ½ large cucumber, peeled, seeded and diced
2 large tomatoes, grilled (page 17) and chopped
3 jalapeño chillies, seeded and chopped
40 g/1½ oz chopped radishes
50 g/2 oz chopped spring onion
15 g/½ oz chopped fresh coriander
2–3 tbsp fresh lemon juice
2–3 tbsp vegetable oil
salt to taste

METHOD

▶ Combine all the ingredients except the salt. Let stand for about 15 minutes, then add salt to taste, and adjust the consistency by adding more lemon juice and oil, if necessary.

20

Sweetcorn Salsa

Makes about 350 g/12 oz

Made with garden-fresh vegetables, sweetcorn salsa is colourful and crunchy, and the jalapeños add gentle heat. For a spicier salsa, don't trim the veins and seeds from the jalapeños. This salsa goes well with grilled seafood or as a garnish for soup. It's also the base for Sweetcorn Salsa Salad with Avocados (page 70). Use fresh sweetcorn whenever possible, but frozen can be substituted.

INGREDIENTS

175 g/6 oz sweetcorn kernels
3 tbsp diced sweet red pepper
3 tbsp diced sweet pepper
2 jalapeño chillies, seeded and minced
25 g/1 oz chopped spring onions
1 large tomato, seeded and chopped
1 tbsp chopped fresh coriander
2 tbsp olive oil
2 tbsp fresh lime juice
¼ tsp ground cumin
¼ tsp salt
pinch of black pepper

METHOD

▶ Put the sweetcorn in a small saucepan with 3 tbsp boiling water. Cook just until tender, about 7 minutes. Drain and leave to cool. Meanwhile, combine all the remaining ingredients. Stir in the sweetcorn. Let stand for about 15 minutes for the flavours to blend, then taste and adjust the seasoning.

Courgette Salsa

21

Makes about 350 g/12 oz

This spicy green relish is dominated by the flavour of coriander, and goes well with roast or grilled meats. If you don't remove any seeds or veins from the jalapeño it will be fairly hot. It should be made no more than 24 hours before eating.

INGREDIENTS

250 g/9 oz shredded raw courgettes
50 g/2 oz finely chopped white onion
1 jalapeño chilli, minced
20 g/¾ oz chopped fresh coriander
1 tbsp olive oil
1 tbsp rice vinegar
¼ tsp salt
1 tsp sugar

METHOD

▶ Mix all the ingredients together. Taste and adjust the seasoning.

Avocado Salsa

Makes about 450 g/1 lb

What distinguishes Avocado Salsa from guacamole is that the avocado is chopped rather than mashed. This is a chunky, spicy salsa that is excellent, if a little messy, with corn chips. It is also delicious with grilled chicken or beef. Use avocados that are perfectly ripe, not the least bit overripe. If you want to prepare this salsa in advance, you may do so, but do not add the avocados until just before serving.

INGREDIENTS

2 large, ripe avocados, peeled, stoned and diced
3 tbsp fresh lime juice
1 tbsp olive oil
75 g/3 oz minced red onion
40 g/1½ oz diced sweet red pepper
3 jalapeño chillies, minced, some seeds included
175 g/6 oz seeded and chopped tomato (about 1 large)
1 tbsp chopped fresh coriander
2 cloves garlic, minced
salt and pepper to taste

METHOD

▶ Mix the avocado chunks with the lime juice and olive oil, then stir in the remaining ingredients. Taste and adjust the seasoning.

22

Olive Salsa

Makes about 575 g/1¼ lb

Here's an unusual salsa that can be the star of a light meal, served over pasta. Try spooning it over salad, or spreading it on slices of French bread, too. There are a lot of strong flavours competing for attention, so the jalapeños won't even be noticeable if you don't include some seeds. If you dislike anchovies, they can be omitted.

INGREDIENTS

200 g/7 oz pitted green olives
75 g/3 oz pitted black olives
3 cloves garlic, finely minced
2 jalapeño chillies, minced, some seeds included
50 g/2 oz finely chopped red onion
50 g/2 oz chopped sweet red pepper
50 g/2 oz anchovy fillets, minced
40 g/1½ oz pine nuts, lightly toasted (see note below), then chopped
2 tbsp olive oil
1 tbsp red wine vinegar

METHOD

▶ Drain the olives and coarsely chop them. Mix them with all the remaining ingredients and let the flavours blend for at least 30 minutes before serving.

To toast pine nuts: Preheat the oven to 150°C/300°F/Gas Mark 2. Spread the pine nuts in a single layer on a small baking sheet or a doubled sheet of foil. Bake for 5 to 10 minutes until they are lightly browned. Watch them closely, as they burn easily.

*Avocado Salsa **(above)** and Olive Salsa **(below)**.*

Tomato-Mint Salsa

Makes about 250 g/9 oz

Mint gives an unusual flavour to this delicious salsa. It is good with fish, especially grilled fish, and also with meat.

INGREDIENTS

4 large tomatoes, cored, halved and seeded
2 cloves garlic, minced
1 tbsp olive oil
1 tbsp fresh lime juice
2 jalapeño chillies, with some seeds and
  veins, minced
15 g/1½ oz chopped fresh mint
¼ tsp salt
pinch of pepper

METHOD

▶ Halve the tomatoes and squeeze out the seeds. Barbecue or grill tomato halves, skin side towards the heat until the skin is partly blackened and slips off easily. Drain off any excess liquid. Chop the tomatoes in a food processor with the garlic, olive oil and lime juice, then stir in the jalapeños and mint. Add the salt and pepper, then taste and adjust the seasoning if necessary.

BONUSES

Looking for something to make your salsa snazzy? Here are a few additions that will go with most tomato salsas.

▶ 50 g/2 oz sliced black olives

▶ 50 g/2 oz finely diced jicama

▶ 175 ml/6 fl oz soured cream

▶ 3 tablespoons beer

▶ a shot of tequila

Tomatillo-Habanero Salsa

Makes about 300 g/11 oz

Roasting the tomatillos and onions gives this salsa extra flavour, but it may be overwhelmed by the habanero chillies, one of the hottest chillies on earth. Fresh habaneros are hard to find, but you can substitute 6 serrano or jalapeño chillies, unseeded. This salsa is good with corn chips, roast meat, or on Huevos Rancheros (page 127).

INGREDIENTS

8 tomatillos, husked and washed
1 small onion, peeled and cut into thick
  slices
4 cloves garlic, unpeeled
3 fresh habanero chillies, unseeded
15 oz/½ oz chopped fresh coriander
1 tbsp fresh lime juice
1 tbsp olive oil
¼ tsp salt

METHOD

▶ Cut the tomatillos in half and roast them with the onion slices and garlic cloves over a barbecue fire. Alternatively, you can grill them, or brown them in a heavy, dry frying pan. The tomatillos and onions should be lightly browned, and the garlic should be soft. Cool the garlic slightly, then peel it, cutting off any scorched parts as they will give the salsa a bitter flavour.

▶ Put the tomatillos, onion and garlic in a food processor with the remaining ingredients. Process until the mixture is chunky, not smooth. If the salsa is too dry, add a little more olive oil, lime juice or water.

Spicy Herb Salsa

Makes about 250 g/9 oz

This salsa, inspired by Italian tomato sauces, uses fresh herbs to create a chunky, flavourful sauce that can be used as a dip, with meat, or over pastas or salads.

INGREDIENTS

15 g/¹/₂ oz chopped fresh basil
1¹/₂ tsp chopped fresh oregano
¹/₂ tsp chopped fresh rosemary
5 cloves garlic, minced
2 tbsp olive oil
4 large tomatoes, seeded and diced
75 g/3 oz chopped onion
2 jalapeño chillies, partially seeded, minced
2 tbsp red wine vinegar
¹/₄ tsp salt

METHOD

▶ If you can start this salsa in advance, mix the fresh herbs, garlic, and olive oil, and let soak for at least an hour. Then combine with the remaining ingredients. Otherwise, combine all the ingredients at once, but let the flavours meld for at least 30 minutes before serving. Taste and adjust the salt.

Cactus Salsa

25

Makes about 450 g/1 lb

In Mexico and the south-western United States, broad, flat cactus paddles are cleaned, cooked and eaten as an ingredient in a number of dishes. Bottled nopales can be found in some specialist shops selling Mexican food. In this recipe, the hot flavour provided by unseeded jalapeños provides a counterpoint to the mild nopales. Use as a dip for corn chips, or mix it into scrambled eggs.

INGREDIENTS

4 large tomatoes, halved and seeded
300 g/1 oz jar of nopales, chopped
25 g/1 oz chopped spring onion
50 g/2 oz chopped white onion
3 jalapeño chillies, unseeded, chopped
3 tbsp chopped fresh coriander
1 tbsp red wine vinegar
1 tbsp fresh lime juice
1 tbsp olive oil
salt and pepper to taste

METHOD

▶ Cut the tomatoes in half and squeeze out the seeds. Cook them under the grill or on a barbecue grid, skins toward the heat, until the skins blacken and slip off easily. Let the tomatoes cool slightly, remove the skins and chop them. Mix with the remaining ingredients. Let stand for 30 minutes, then taste and adjust the seasoning.

Chilli plants growing in the fields of New Mexico.

Barbecued Salsa

Makes about 350 g/12 oz

All the main ingredients in this salsa are barbecued, giving it a delicious smoky taste. The poblano chillies add mild to moderate heat. A grill tray for small items is a necessity or you'll lose the garlic and most of the tomato in the coals. If you don't have one, you may grill the vegetables rather than barbecue them, but the flavour will not be as good. Remember to keep the skins of the tomatoes and chillies facing the heat source.

INGREDIENTS

5 large tomatoes, halved and seeded
1 small white onion, peeled and cut into
    thick slices
3 poblano chillies, quartered lengthwise
4 cloves garlic, unpeeled
1 tbsp fresh lime juice
salt and pepper to taste

METHOD

▶ Halve the tomatoes and place them, cut side up, on a grill tray. Add the chillies skin side down. It doesn't matter which way you turn the onion and garlic. When the barbecue flames have died down and the coals are glowing, place the tray of vegetables directly over the coals.

▶ Turn the garlic frequently and remove it as soon as it softens, as it will turn bitter and mar the taste of the salsa if it scorches. When the garlic is cooked enough to handle, peel it.

▶ The skin on the chillies should brown and blister, but the flesh must not burn. Don't expect the skin to blister evenly. As soon as each piece of chilli is done, put it in a plastic bag and close the top.

▶ The onion slices should brown slightly. Then turn them over and let the other side brown. Again, don't let them burn.

▶ Cook the tomatoes until the skin browns and slides off easily. It's fine if the flesh browns a little. When the tomatoes are cooked, put them in a bowl or colander where liquid can drain off.

▶ Allow the chillies to steam in the bag for about 10 minutes. Then with a sharp knife, peel off the blistered skin. It's fine if a few bits of charred skin remain. Because poblanos have a tendency to get stringy, cut each piece into a few short pieces.

▶ Put chillies, peeled garlic, onion slices and drained tomatoes in a blender or food processor with lime juice and a little salt and pepper. Process until the vegetables are well chopped, but not to the point where the mixture is completely smooth. Taste and adjust the salt and pepper.

26

Black Bean Salsa

Makes about 350 g/12 oz

Black Bean Salsa has an excellent mixture of textures and flavours, producing a spicy relish that goes well with fish, meat, and eggs. You may use canned black beans or soak and cook dried beans. You can also use kidney beans. With canned beans, this is a very easy-to-make dish.

INGREDIENTS

450 g/1 lb can of black or kidney beans,
    rinsed and drained
50 g/2 oz chopped sweet red pepper
3 spring onions, chopped
2 chipotle chillies, minced
3 tbsp chopped fresh coriander
1¹/₂ tsp chopped fresh oregano or ¹/₂ tsp dried
1 tbsp olive oil
2 tbsp fresh lime juice
salt to taste

METHOD

▶ Combine all the ingredients. Let stand for about 30 minutes, then taste and adjust the seasoning.

*Barbecued Salsa (**above**) and Black Bean Salsa (**below**).*

Coriander-Chilli Pesto

Makes about 250 g/9 oz

This spicy pesto uses traditional salsa ingredients, although its texture is different. It is simple and delicious. Spoon it over pasta, steamed vegetables or meat.

INGREDIENTS

75 g/3 oz fresh coriander leaves
5 cloves garlic, peeled
1 jalapeño chilli
2 poblano chillies, grilled (page 12) and peeled
½ large red onion
6 tbsp olive oil
50 g/2 oz walnuts
½ tsp salt

METHOD

► Put all the ingredients in a food processor and process until almost smooth.

Kitchen Sink Guacamole

28

Makes about 575 g/1¼ lb

This guacamole is a purist's nightmare, but never mind, it has a great taste.

INGREDIENTS

3 large avocados, crudely mashed (but not puréed)
2 tomatoes, seeded and chopped
40 g/1½ oz chopped onion
2 jalapeño chillies, chopped and partly seeded
2 tbsp fresh lime juice
6 rashers bacon, cooked and crumbled
40 g/1½ oz sliced black olives
salt and pepper to taste

METHOD

► Combine all the ingredients, then taste and adjust the seasoning. Serve immediately.

Radish Salsa

Makes about 350 g/12 oz

Serve this hot radish relish as a side dish with grilled meats, especially pork.

INGREDIENTS

40 g/1½ oz finely chopped red onion
1½ tsp crushed dried chilli
4 tbsp white wine vinegar
225 g/8 oz thinly sliced radishes (about 2 bunches)
3 tbsp chopped fresh coriander
1 tbsp olive oil
pinch of salt

METHOD

► Combine the onion, chilli and vinegar, and let soak for at least 1 hour. Mix in the remaining ingredients.

Roast Sweetcorn Salsa

Makes about 575 g/1¼ lb

Because some of the vegetables are barbecued, this sauce has a smoky flavour and a very different texture from the preceding Sweetcorn Salsa. It is a more sophisticated recipe that goes well with grilled chicken and meat, and is also the base for a delicious crab chowder (page 78). Without jalapeño seeds, it is moderately spicy.

INGREDIENTS

4 large ears of sweetcorn, in husks
3 large tomatoes
1 poblano chilli
2 cloves garlic, unpeeled
½ sweet red pepper
50 g/2 oz chopped spring onions
2 jalapeño chillies, seeded and minced
2 tbsp chopped fresh coriander
1 tsp chopped fresh oregano or ¼ tsp dried
3 tbsp olive oil
salt and pepper to taste

METHOD

► Carefully peel the sweetcorn husks back and remove the silks. Pull the husks back up and tie at the top with string if necessary. Soak the sweetcorn in water for 30 minutes, then drain, place in a 200°C/400°F/Gas Mark 6 oven, and roast for 20 minutes. Leave until cool enough to handle.

► While sweetcorn is cooling, preheat the grill. Core the tomatoes, cut them in half and squeeze out the seeds. Place them cut side down on a flameproof baking sheet.

► Cut the poblano chilli in quarters lengthwise, removing the stem, veins and seeds. Cut the half of the sweet red pepper in half again lengthwise. Place the chilli and the red pepper on the baking sheet, skin side up. If the chilli or pepper pieces don't lie nearly flat, cut them into additional pieces so that the skin is fairly evenly exposed to the broiler. Put the unpeeled garlic cloves on the baking sheet too. The ingredients will cook at different speeds, so watch them carefully.

► The tomato skin should darken and loosen enough so that it will slip off easily. The skin on the poblano chilli and the red pepper should be almost completely blackened. The garlic cloves should soften. Remove each piece when it is ready. Place the chilli and the pepper into a plastic bag or make a foil pouch. After 10 minutes, remove the chilli and pepper from the bag and cut off the blackened skin, leaving just a few bits of skin on the flesh for colour and flavour. Slip the skins off the tomatoes and drain off the excess juices. Peel the garlic cloves. Chop the tomatoes, chilli, red pepper and garlic, and put them in a medium bowl.

► Remove the husks from the sweetcorn and roast the ears over glowing coals or under a grill. Turn them frequently so that bits of the kernels are browned on all sides. Do not allow the sweetcorn to brown completely.

► Remove the sweetcorn from the grid or grill and leave until cool enough to handle. With a sharp knife, cut the kernels off the cobs and add to the vegetables. Stir in the spring onions, jalapeños, coriander, oregano, olive oil, salt and pepper. Taste and adjust the seasoning.

29

In this mass of red and green chillies you can see how the chillies ripen from green to red.

cooked salsas

Basic Cooked Salsa
Green Chilli Sauce
Red Chilli Sauce
Chipotle Salsa
Salsa Verde
Garlic Salsa
Black Bean-Sweetcorn Salsa
Fiery Habanero Salsa

Winter Salsa I
Winter Salsa II
Winter Salsa III

Basic Cooked Salsa

Makes about 500 g/18 oz

This simple cooked salsa is good with corn chips or as a sauce over eggs or Mexican food. With a few jalapeño seeds included, it is fairly hot. You may use unpeeled tomatoes, but if you wish to remove the skin, dip the tomatoes in boiling water for 30 seconds. The skins should slip off easily.

INGREDIENTS

450 g/1 lb seeded, chopped tomatoes
2 cloves minced garlic
75 g/3 oz finely chopped onion
4 jalapeño chillies, chopped, with some seeds included
1 tbsp cider vinegar
1 tsp fresh oregano or ¼ tsp dried
salt to taste

METHOD

▶ In a medium saucepan, simmer the tomatoes, garlic and onion for 10 to 15 minutes, uncovered, to evaporate excess liquid from the tomatoes. Add the jalapeños, vinegar and oregano, and simmer for 5 minutes more. Add salt to taste.

Green Chilli Sauce

32

Makes about 350 g/12 oz

This delicious sauce is traditionally made with green New Mexico chillies. However, since fresh New Mexico chillies are hard to find, you can substitute mild Anaheim chillies and add several jalapeño or serrano chillies to boost the heat. This sauce is a key ingredient in enchiladas, but can also be served with tacos, corn chips, and many other dishes.

INGREDIENTS

6 green New Mexico chillies (or 6 Anaheim chillies plus 3 to 4 jalapeño or serrano chillies)
3 cloves garlic
4 tomatillos, husked and halved
2 1-cm/½-in thick slices white onion, peeled
¼ tsp salt
250 ml/8 fl oz water or chicken stock

METHOD

▶ Roast the chillies, garlic, tomatillos and onion as described on page 26 under Barbecued Salsa. Peel and seed the chillies, and cut them into strips across their width. Peel the garlic. Cut the tomatillos and onions into chunks. Purée the chillies, garlic, tomatillos and onion with the salt and 6 tbsp water or chicken stock. Put the purée in a saucepan with the remaining water or stock and simmer until it reaches the desired consistency. Taste and adjust the salt.

The warm colour of red chillies lends a wonderful richness to sauces.

Red Chilli Sauce

Makes 500 g/18 oz

This hot chilli sauce is used most often to make enchiladas, but it can also be added to meat or beans, or served as a table sauce to be spooned over tacos, eggs, or other dishes. For less heat, substitute dried California chillies for some of the New Mexico chillies. Or for variety, use a combination of New Mexico, California, ancho, or other dried chillies.

INGREDIENTS

12 dried New Mexico chillies
600 ml/1 pint beef stock
4 cloves garlic, minced
75 g/3 oz chopped onion
½ tsp dried oregano
¼ tsp salt

METHOD

▶ Preheat the oven to 120°C/250°F/Gas Mark ½. Place the chillies on an ungreased baking sheet and bake for 6 to 8 minutes, shaking once or twice, until they are brittle. Do not allow them to blacken or they will be bitter. Remove the chillies and let stand until they are cool enough to handle. Remove the stems and as many of the seeds as desired.

▶ Bring 1 litre/1¾ pints water to the boil in a medium saucepan. Crumble the chillies into the boiling water and simmer for 20 to 30 minutes until soft. Drain off the water and discard. Put the chillies into a food processor with about 6 tbsp of the beef stock and purée. Strain to remove the skins. Put the skins back in the food processor with another 6 tbsp beef stock. Purée again and strain. Discard the skins.

▶ Add the remaining ingredients to the strained sauce and purée. Return the sauce to the heat, and simmer until it reaches the desired consistency.

33

Clockwise from the top: *Basic Cooked Salsa, Green Chilli Sauce and Red Chilli Sauce.*

Chipotle Salsa

Makes about 350 g/12 oz

This hot, smoky salsa gets its marvellous flavour from dried chipotle chillies. It is excellent with corn chips, on **Huevos Rancheros (page 127)**, tacos or with meat.

INGREDIENTS

4 dried chipotle chillies
450 g/1 lb seeded and chopped tomatoes
75 g/3 oz chopped onion
75 g/3 oz chopped sweet pepper
salt to taste

METHOD

► Remove the seeds and stems, and put the chipotle chillies in a small, heat-resistant bowl and pour 150 ml/¼ pint boiling water over them. Let them soak until they are pliable, about 30 minutes. If chillies are very dry and brittle, gently simmer them in the water. Remove the stems, then put the chillies and the soaking water in a food processor and purée.

► Put the chipotle purée in a small saucepan with all the remaining ingredients. Simmer until any excess liquid evaporates, 15 to 20 minutes. If the chipotles did not purée easily, or if you want a smooth sauce for dipping, briefly process the salsa again.

Note: You may also use chipotle chillies canned in adobo sauce. Skip the soaking in hot water. Coarsely chop the chipotles before adding them to the salsa, then process after the salsa is cooked. Without the soaking water, there will not be as much excess liquid, and the salsa will not have to cook quite as long.

Salsa Verde

Makes about 350 g/12 oz

Fresh tomatillos give Salsa Verde its green colour. It tastes best when it is very spicy, so include the jalapeño seeds and veins. Use as you would a basic tomato salsa.

INGREDIENTS

450 g/1 lb tomatillos (about 20), husked and washed
2 jalapeño chillies, unseeded, chopped
1 clove garlic, minced
1 medium onion, chopped
15 g/½ oz chopped fresh coriander
1 tbsp fresh lemon juice
½ tsp salt
1–2 tbsp vegetable oil
1–2 tsp sugar (optional)

METHOD

▶ Add the tomatillos to a pan of boiling water and simmer for 10 minutes. Drain, and transfer to a blender or food processor. Process until finely chopped.

▶ Mix all the remaining ingredients except the oil and sugar with the tomatillos. Heat the oil in a frying pan, add the salsa and fry briefly, then simmer until the excess liquid has reduced, about 10 minutes. Taste. If the tomatillos were too green and the salsa is tart, add the sugar.

Garlic Salsa

3 5

Makes about 200 g/7 oz

Use this pungent sauce as you would any other tomato-based salsa – with corn chips, over eggs, on tacos, or with meat.

INGREDIENTS

3 large tomatoes, peeled, seeded and diced
75 g/3 oz chopped onion
1 japaleño chilli, trimmed of all but a few seeds and veins
¼–½ tsp salt
12 cloves garlic, minced
1 tbsp chopped fresh basil or 1 tsp dried

METHOD

▶ Simmer the tomatoes, onion, jalapeño and ¼ tsp salt for about 10 minutes to evaporate excess liquid. Add the garlic and basil, and cook for another 2 to 3 minutes. Taste and adjust the salt if necessary.

Black Bean-Sweetcorn Salsa

Makes about 900 g/2 lb

Made with roasted sweetcorn and three kinds of chillies, this is a hearty salsa that fills your mouth with a symphony of flavours. It is delicious warm with grilled salmon. Serve it on the side or as a topping for other fish, chicken or pork, or as a vegetarian main dish. At a pinch, you can substitute 350 g/12 oz of canned black beans, rinsed and drained, but there is no doubt that the warm, cooked dried beans have a better flavour.

Ingredients

175 g/6 oz dried black beans
3 large ears of sweetcorn or 5 small ears, still in their husks
1 small onion, peeled and quartered
4 cloves garlic
2 ancho chillies, halved and seeded
2 large tomatoes, cored, halved and seeded
2 Anaheim chillies, halved and seeded
75 g/3 oz chopped red onion
50 g/2 oz chopped spring onion
2 jalapeño chillies, seeded and minced
1 tsp cumin
1–3 tsp salt

36

Method

► Sort the dried beans, removing any pebbles. Put the beans in a medium saucepan and add 750 ml/1¼ pints of water. Bring to the boil and boil for 2 minutes, then cover the pan, turn off the heat and let stand for 1 hour.

► Meanwhile, prepare the sweetcorn. Carefully peel back the husks and remove the silks, then pull the husks back up around the sweetcorn. Soak the corn in cool water for 30 minutes. If you are going to barbecue the corn, start a charcoal fire.

► Drain and rinse the beans. Put them in a large saucepan, add 750 ml/1¼ pints water, the quartered onion and 2 cloves garlic, peeled and crushed. Bring to the boil, reduce the heat and simmer, uncovered, until the beans are tender and the liquid has evaporated, 1 to 1½ hours. Check occasionally, adding more water if needed.

► While the beans are cooking, prepare the ancho chillies and roast the vegetables. Reconstitute the ancho chilli halves in 4 tbsp boiling water in a small, heat-resistant bowl. Leave to soak for 20 minutes, stirring once or twice to be sure all of the chilli is softened. Purée the chillies and their soaking liquid in a blender, then add this purée to the beans while they are simmering.

► Drain the sweetcorn. If you are using a barbecue, the coals should be glowing, and no longer flaming. Add a few more coals to extend the barbecuing time, then place the sweetcorn at the side of the barbecue grid, not directly over the coals. Cover the grid and let the sweetcorn roast for 20 minutes. Alternatively, place the sweetcorn on a baking tin and cook in a preheated 200°C/400°F/Gas Mark 6 oven for 20 minutes. Remove the sweetcorn and leave until cool enough to handle. If you are not using the barbecue, turn on the grill. Remove the husks from the sweetcorn and place the sweetcorn on the grid over the coals, or under the grill, turning so that the kernels are lightly browned in spots. Do not let it brown all over or it will be too dry. Remove from the heat and leave until cool enough to handle. Cut the kernels from the cobs.

► Roast the tomatoes and Anaheim chillies on the grid over charcoal or under the grill. Always make sure the skins face the heat source. Cook until tomato skins are browned and slip off easily, and until chilli skins are almost completely blackened. Put the chillies in a small bag or in an envelope of foil for 10 minutes. Remove the skin from the chillies (it's fine if you leave a little bit of blackened skin on) and slip the skin from the tomatoes. Chop the tomatoes and chillies.

► Remove the beans from the heat, discarding the onion and garlic. Mince the remaining 2 cloves garlic and add to the beans with the roast sweetcorn, chopped tomatoes and Anaheim chillies. Stir in the remaining ingredients, including 1 tsp salt. Taste and add more salt if needed. Serve warm or at room temperature.

Clockwise from the top: Black Bean-Sweetcorn Salsa, Fiery Habanero Salsa (page 38) and Winter Salsa I (page 38).

Fiery Habanero Salsa

Makes about 175 g/6 oz

This salsa, which uses a single dried habanero chilli, is the hottest in the book, and tolerable only to those whose nerve endings are already irreparably damaged by capsaicin. It is excellent with almost everything – corn chips, eggs, meat or tacos. Just be sure to have lots of milk available for relief. See picture on page 37.

INGREDIENTS

1 whole dried habanero chilli
225 g/8 oz tomatoes, skinned, seeded and
  chopped
75 g/3 oz chopped red onion
2 cloves garlic, minced
15 g/¹/₂ oz chopped fresh coriander
1 tbsp cider vinegar
1 tbsp olive oil
¹/₄ tsp salt

METHOD

▶ Remove and discard the stem of the habanero and then reconstitute it in 150 ml/ ¹/₄ pint boiling water for about 30 minutes. Then chop coarsely. Put the habanero and its soaking water in a small saucepan with the tomato, onion and garlic. Simmer for 10 to 15 minutes, until the excess liquid has evaporated. Add all the remaining ingredients and cook for 2 minutes longer. Put the salsa in a food processor or blender and process until the habanero is well chopped, but the salsa is not completely puréed.

Winter Salsa I

OUT-OF-SEASON SALSA

So it's January and you have a craving for salsa and cornchips, but the only tomatoes in the shops are hard and flavourless. As for fresh chillies, there are none. Don't worry; you can still satisfy that craving.

Canned tomatoes, especially Italian plum tomatoes, are better than unripe fresh tomatoes. Canned chillies are not a good substitute for fresh ones – unless they are chipotle chillies – but dried chillies are.

The next three recipes for salsa use ingredients that can be found in the grocery shops year-round. You won't mistake them for Salsa Cruda, but they're good.

Makes 300 g/11 oz

This moderately spicy store cupboard salsa (see picture on page 37) is based on canned tomatoes and dried ancho chillies, making it suitable for the winter months when good, flavoursome, fresh ingredients are hard to come by. Serve with corn chips, on tacos and other tortilla dishes, or with eggs.

INGREDIENTS

2 ancho chillies (sometimes labelled
  pasillas)
400 g/14 oz can whole tomatoes
2 cloves garlic, minced
75 g/3 oz chopped onion
2–3 tsp dried coriander
1 tsp sugar
¹/₄ tsp salt

METHOD

▶ Cut open the ancho chillies and remove the stems and most of the seeds. Cut the chillies into 2.5-cm/1-in pieces – this will make it easier to process the salsa. Put the chilli pieces in a small, heat-resistant bowl and pour about 6 tbsp of boiling water over the chillies. Use as little water as possible, and stir to be sure all the pieces are covered with water. Let them stand for 20 minutes, or longer if the chillies seem particularly dry.

▶ Drain the chillies, discarding the water. Put the chilli pieces in a blender or food processor with about half the tomatoes and their juice. Process until the chillies are well chopped. Chop the remaining tomatoes by hand and put in a small saucepan with the chilli mixture and the remaining ingredients. Simmer for 10 minutes or so until the excess liquid has evaporated.

Winter Salsa II

Makes about 250 g/9 oz

Canned tomatoes and chipotle chillies are the main ingredients of this hot, smoky salsa. The chillies are canned in adobo sauce, some of which is added to the salsa.

INGREDIENTS

400 g/14 oz can whole or chopped (not
   stewed) tomatoes
3 chipotle chillies canned in adobo sauce,
   plus 1 tbsp adobo sauce
75 g/3 oz chopped onion
$^1/_2$ tsp dried oregano
salt to taste

METHOD

▶ Process the tomatoes, chipotle chillies and adobo sauce in a food processor, leaving the mixture a litle chunky. Put the salsa in a small saucepan and add the onions and oregano. Simmer for 10 minutes, then add salt to taste.

Winter Salsa III

Makes about 175 g/6 oz

This fiery New Mexico salsa uses crushed dried chillies to give it its heat. Add another tablespoon of chilli flakes to make it even hotter.

INGREDIENTS

40 g/1$^1/_2$ oz chopped onion
2 tbsp red chilli flakes
1 tsp dried oregano
4 tbsp red wine vinegar
400 g/14 oz can whole tomatoes
$^1/_4$ tsp ground cumin
$^1/_4$ to $^1/_2$ tsp salt

METHOD

▶ Combine the onion, chilli flakes, oregano and vinegar. Let the mixture soak for at least an hour. Chop, but don't completely purée, the tomatoes in a blender or food processor. Put the tomatoes in a small saucepan with the vinegar mixture, cumin and salt. Bring to the boil and simmer for 10 minutes, or longer if needed, to reduce the excess liquid. Taste and adjust the seasoning.

39

*In certain parts of America, the chilli crop is celebrated each year
with festivals, parades and "cook-offs".*

fruit
salsas

Avocado-Mango Salsa
Pineapple-Ginger Salsa
Tropical Salsa
Barbecued Mango-Habanero Salsa
Cranberry-Papaya Salsa
Nectarine Salsa
Jicama-Peach Salsa
Mango Salsa
Black Bean-Papaya Salsa

Avocado-Mango Salsa

Makes about 350 g/12 oz

The rich, pleasantly sweet combination of avocado and mango is made piquant with hot serrano chillies and red onion. Serve with meat, poultry or fish.

INGREDIENTS

1 mango, peeled, stoned and diced
1 avocado, peeled, stoned and diced
2 serrano chillies, unseeded, minced
75 g/3 oz chopped red onion
3 tbsp chopped fresh coriander
2 tbsp fresh lime juice
2 tbsp orange juice
pinch of ground cumin

METHOD

► Combine all the ingredients.

Pineapple-Ginger Salsa

Makes about 575 g/1¼ lb

42

Barbecuing the pineapple mellows its acidity and provides a sweet counterpoint to the sharp kick of jalapeño and fresh ginger. This salsa goes well with meat, especially pork, but it's so good you may just want to eat it straight from the bowl. It should be eaten the same day it is prepared.

INGREDIENTS

2 or 3 2.5-cm/1-in thick slices of fresh pineapple, unpeeled
75 g/3 oz chopped sweet red pepper
75 g/3 oz chopped red onion
2 jalapeño chillies, unseeded, chopped
2–3 tsp finely minced fresh ginger
1 tbsp rice vinegar

METHOD

► Cook the pineapple slices over glowing embers until they are marked with brown lines from the grid and show spots of brown, 3 to 5 minutes a side. Let the pineapple cool slightly, then pare off the peel and cut out the tough core. Dice the flesh to make about 275 g/10 oz of pineapple. Mix with the remaining ingredients. Let stand for at least 30 minutes to allow the flavours to blend.

Tropical Salsa

Makes about 300 g/11 oz

There's a definite whiff of the tropics in this salsa, which includes mango, pineapple and mint. Make it no more than a few hours before you plan to eat, and serve it as an accompaniment to meat. I use it to dress up plain roast turkey.

INGREDIENTS

1 ripe mango, peeled, stoned and diced
75 g/3 oz fresh pineapple, peeled and diced
2 tbsp chopped fresh mint
2 tbsp chopped fresh coriander
40 g/1½ oz chopped red onion
1 serrano chilli, minced
1 sweet Italian or other mild chilli, seeded and minced
1 tbsp orange juice
1 tbsp olive oil
¼–½ tsp ground cumin
salt to taste

METHOD

► Combine all the ingredients. Let stand for at least 20 minutes, then taste and adjust the seasoning if necessary.

Clockwise from the top: *Avocado-Mango Salsa, Tropical Salsa and Pineapple-Ginger Salsa.*

Barbecued Mango-Habanero Salsa

Makes about 300 g/11 oz

This sweet-hot salsa, which goes well with meat or poultry, is an unusual combination of barbecued mango, sweet onions, and fiery habanero chillies. Barbecuing intensifies the sweetness of the mango, which decreases the habanero's fire. It is only moderately hot if you remove the veins and seeds from the habanero, but incendiary if you leave them in. If you cannot find habanero chillies, substitute 3 serrano chillies. It is important to use a special grill tray, otherwise, you will almost certainly lose some of the mango in the barbecue coals.

Ingredients

2 ripe but firm mangoes
1 large or 2 small mild, sweet onions
1 habanero chilli, minced
3 tbsp minced fresh coriander
2 tbsp fresh lime juice
1 tbsp rice vinegar
pinch of salt

Method

► Cut the mangoes into wedges but do not peel them, because the rind will make them easier to handle as they soften during cooking.

Peel and cut a large onion into thick slices, or cut small onions in half. Put the mangoes and onions on a lightly oiled grill tray, and cook until a few brown spots appear on the mango flesh. Turn the mangoes. The onions should be turned when they are a little browner than the mangoes, but not completely brown. Remove and let cool.

► Cut the rind off the mango slices and cut the flesh into 5-mm/¼-in dice. The fruit should be very juicy. Chop the onions and add to the mangoes with the remaining ingredients.

Cranberry-Papaya Salsa

Makes about 575 g/1¼ lb

Here's a spicy twist on the traditional cranberry sauce served with roast turkey. Two unseeded jalapeño chillies give it an unexpected bite. With slight adjustments, this salsa can be served cooked or raw. For a sharper, rough-textured relish, serve it raw. The cooked version is sweeter and smoother.

Ingredients

½ orange, unpeeled
½ medium onion, peeled
2 jalapeño chillies, stems removed, unseeded
300 g/11 oz fresh or frozen cranberries
1 tbsp fresh lime juice
75 g/3 oz honey
*1 papaya, peeled, seeded and cut into
   5-mm/¼-in dice*

Uncooked salsa

► Cut the orange and onion halves into a few chunks, and remove the orange seeds. Put the orange and onion in a food processor and chop coarsely. Cut the jalapeños into 3 or 4 pieces and add them to the orange and onion, together with the cranberries, lime juice and honey. Process until well chopped. Do not process so long that the salsa becomes liquefied or turns into a paste. Remove from the processor and mix with the papaya. Taste and adjust the lime juice and honey, if needed.

Cooked salsa

Ingredients as listed but with:
100 g/4 oz honey
2 tbsp water

► Cut and process the orange and onion as directed above. Add the cranberries, lime juice, honey and water. Do not add the jalapeños. Process, then transfer to a small saucepan and simmer for about 10 minutes, until the water has evaporated and the sauce is ruby-coloured. Check the sweetness, and add more honey, if desired. Remove from the heat and let cool. Mince the jalapeños and add to the cooled salsa with the papaya.

Nectarine Salsa

Makes about 175 g/6 oz

Sweet nectarines are mixed with onion and fresh chilli, then sprinkled with chilli powder to make a spicy-sweet salsa that is delicious with seafood or chicken. It can be made several hours in advance.

INGREDIENTS

3 ripe nectarines, peeled, stoned and chopped
4 tbsp finely chopped spring onion
1 jalapeño or serrano chilli, finely chopped, some seeds included
40 g/1½ oz finely chopped sweet red pepper
2 tbsp chopped fresh basil
2 tbsp fresh lime juice
¼ tsp chilli powder
salt and pepper to taste

METHOD

▶ With a fork, mash about 2 tablespoons of the chopped nectarine. Stir in the rest of the nectarine and the remaining ingredients. Let stand for about 15 minutes, then taste and adjust the seasoning.

Jicama-Peach Salsa

Makes about 450 g/1 lb

Jicama-Peach Salsa is sweet, moderately hot and crunchy. It makes an excellent side dish.

INGREDIENTS

175 g/6 oz finely diced jicama (about ½ medium jicama, peeled)
100 g/4 oz chopped red onion
50 g/2 oz chopped sweet red pepper
2 medium peaches, peeled, stoned and chopped
2 jalapeño chillies, unseeded, chopped
2–3 tbsp fresh lime juice
½ tsp chilli powder
1 tbsp chopped fresh basil

METHOD

▶ Combine all the ingredients.

45

Fresh fruits and vegetables combine well with the spicy tastes of chillies in salsas.

Mango Salsa

Makes about 350 g/12 oz

Mango is a popular ingredient in salsas from the Caribbean and the Philippines because its cool sweetness provides a perfect complement to the spiciness of the chillies.

INGREDIENTS

2 mangoes, peeled, stoned and diced
75 g/3 oz chopped red onion
75 g/3 oz chopped sweet red pepper
2 jalapeño chillies, seeded and chopped
3 tbsp fresh lime juice

METHOD

▶ Combine all the ingredients.

Black Bean-Papaya Salsa

Makes about 450 g/1 lb

46

This beautiful, spicy-sweet salsa is spiked with fresh ginger. It goes well with chicken, fish and meat, especially pork.

INGREDIENTS

450 g/1 lb can black beans, rinsed and
*   drained*
1 papaya, peeled, seeded and diced
2 poblano chillies, roasted (page 12),
*   peeled and chopped*
75 g/3 oz sweet red pepper, chopped
75 g/3 oz chopped red onion
15 g/½ oz chopped fresh coriander
1 tsp finely minced fresh ginger
3 tbsp fresh lime juice
1 tsp crushed dried red chilli
salt and pepper to taste

METHOD

▶ Combine all the ingredients. Let stand for 30 minutes, then taste and adjust the seasoning.

*Black Bean-Papaya Salsa **(above)** and Mango Salsa **(below)**.*

appetizers

Triple-Treat Salsa Spread
Prosciutto Prawns
Hot Bean Dip
Chorizo-Bean Dip
Chicken-Avocado Salsa Spread
Nachos
Layered Fiesta Dip
Seafood Salsa Spread
Homemade Tortilla Chips
Empanadas

Chilli con Queso
Tostaditas

Triple-Treat Salsa Spread

Makes about 675 g/1½ lb

This party dish incorporates three different salsas and cream cheese into a layered spread that is absolutely delicious. It should be made at least 4 hours in advance of serving, and improves if prepared 24 hours in advance. It is easier to make if you chill the spread for about 30 minutes after adding each layer. For a simpler dish, you can omit the Avocado Salsa, or spoon more tomato salsa over the top instead. Serve it with biscuits.

INGREDIENTS

450 g/1 lb cream cheese
2 tbsp milk
50 g/2 oz tomato-based salsa, such as Basic Cooked Salsa (page 32)
Coriander-Chilli Pesto (page 28)
200 g/7 oz Avocado Salsa (page 22)

METHOD

▶ Select a straight-sided or nearly straight-sided dish that is about 15 cm/6 in in diameter and at least 5 cm/2 in deep; a soufflé dish is perfect. Line the bottom and sides with cling film, smoothing out the film as much as possible. Leave some cling film overhanging the sides of the dish.

▶ Beat half the cream cheese with the milk so it is easily spreadable but not runny. Spread this mixture as evenly as possible over the bottom of the dish. Chill for 30 minutes. Spread the Coriander-Chilli Pesto evenly over the cream cheese and chill. Beat the remaining cream cheese with the tomato salsa and spread it over the Coriander-Chilli Pesto. Chill for at least 4 hours.

▶ Just before serving, make the Avocado Salsa. (Or make the Avocado Salsa in advance and add the avocado at the last minute.) Place a serving dish on top of the dish containing the spread and, holding the 2 dishes tightly together, invert them both. Gently pull the cling film so that the spread drops onto the serving dish, remove the top dish, and carefully peel off the cling film. Spoon the Avocado Salsa over the top of the spread. Serve immediately.

50

St George's market in Grenada. Salsas are very much a part of the cuisine of the Caribbean.

Prosciutto Prawns

Makes 4 servings

Prosciutto is Italian ham that has been cured in a spiced brine, then air-dried and aged for about a year. Because its flavour is so concentrated by this process, only a paper-thin slice is needed. In this simple but elegant appetizer, fruit and prawns are wrapped in prosciutto and topped with Mango Salsa. If serving as a first course, allow 3 per person.

INGREDIENTS

12 medium to large prawns, cooked and cleaned
2 tbsp fresh lime juice
3 fresh figs, quartered, or 12 small wedges of honeydew melon
6 large or 12 small slices of prosciutto
175 g/6 oz Mango Salsa (page 46)

METHOD

▶ Toss the prawns with the lime juice. Let stand for 5 minutes, then drain off the juice if necessary.

▶ Pair each prawn with a fig quarter or melon wedge. Cut large slices of prosciutto in half lengthwise. Wrap prosciutto around the fruit and prawns. Top with Mango Salsa.

51

Hot Bean Dip

Makes about 675 g/1½ lb

This easy recipe uses canned refried beans as a base, then adds spices, cheese, and Salsa Cruda to make it a flavourful dip. Serve it hot, with thick corn chips for dipping.

INGREDIENTS

250 g/9 oz canned refried beans
250 g/9 oz Salsa Cruda (pages 18–19)
175 g/6 oz grated Cheddar cheese
¼ tsp ground cumin
¼ tsp dried oregano
salt if needed (depending on the saltiness of the beans)
40 g/1½ oz sliced black olives
2 tbsp chopped spring onions

METHOD

▶ Heat the beans in a pan until bubbly. Add the salsa, 100 g/4 oz cheese, the cumin and oregano. Stir until the cheese has melted, then taste and add salt if needed. Spoon into a heat-resistant serving dish and garnish with the remaining cheese, the olives and onions.

Note: If desired, garnish first with cheese only. Put the bowl in a 180°C/350°F/Gas Mark 5, oven for a few minutes until the cheese is melted. Then garnish with the olives and spring onions.

52

Chorizo-Bean Dip

Makes about 575 g/1¼ lb

Black beans puréed with spicy chorizo sausage
and salsa make a delicious hot dip for corn chips.
The leftovers are so good in omelettes,
empanadas (page 60), and tostaditas (page 63)
that you'll want to make a double batch.

INGREDIENTS

175 g/6 oz dried black beans
about 150 g/5 oz chorizo sausage
75 g/3 oz chopped onion
1 to 2 tsp salt
175 g/6 oz Salsa Cruda I (page 18)

METHOD

► Sort through the beans and discard any
pebbles or other debris. Soak the beans
overnight in 1 litre/1¾ pints water, or bring
the beans and water to the boil, boil for 2
minutes, then turn off the heat and let stand,
covered, for 1 hour. Drain and rinse the beans.
Put the beans in a medium saucepan with 1
litre/1¾ pints water. Bring to the boil, reduce
the heat and simmer.

► Crumble the chorizo into a small frying pan
and fry until browned, 5 to 7 minutes. Tilt the
pan to drain the grease, remove the meat with
a slotted spoon and add to the beans. Discard
all but 1 tbsp grease in the pan. Reheat, and
add the chopped onion. Sauté for 5 minutes,
then add to the beans. Continue simmering
the beans until tender, adding a little more
water, if needed, so that there is still some
cooking liquid left when the beans are done.
The total cooking time should be 1 to 1½
hours. Stir in 1 tsp salt.

► Remove the pan from the heat and set aside
about 100 g/4 oz beans. Purée the rest in a
blender or food processor, then stir in the
whole beans and the salsa. Taste and add more
salt if necessary. Serve warm.

Chicken-Avocado Salsa Spread

Makes about 300 g/11 oz

This spread is more delicately flavoured than most of the recipes in this book. If you want it to have more kick, add a chopped jalapeño, seeds and veins included, or some hot pepper sauce. You can make the spread in advance, but don't add the avocado until the last minute. Marinating and barbecuing the chicken, as on page 110, will give the spread additional flavour, but any method of cooking the chicken will do.

INGREDIENTS

150 g/5 oz finely chopped cooked chicken
175 g/6 oz Grilled Salsa (page 26)
1 large avocado, peeled, stoned and mashed
1 tbsp lemon juice
salt to taste
coriander leaves or chopped spring onion for garnish (optional)

METHOD

► Combine all the ingredients and garnish with coriander or spring onion, if desired. Serve with biscuits.

Nachos

54

Makes 3 to 4 servings

Homemade nachos are easy to make, and with real cheese and lots of extras they're better than most commercial versions. The joy of homemade nachos is that you can prepare them to suit your own taste. This deluxe version calls for tomatoes, avocados, olives, spring onions, and salsa.

INGREDIENTS

300 g/11 oz packet of tortilla chips
350 g/12 oz grated Cheddar cheese
2 or 3 jalapeño chillies, fresh or canned, cut crosswise into thin slices
2 medium tomatoes, seeded and chopped
40 g/1½ oz chopped spring onions
50–75 g/2–3 oz black olives, stoned and sliced
1 large ripe avocado, peeled, stoned, and diced, or Avocado Salsa (page 22) or Guacamole (page 17)
175 g/6 oz tomato-based salsa, such as Basic Cooked Salsa (page 32)

METHOD

► Preheat the oven to 200°C/400°F/Gas Mark 6. Mound the tortilla chips on 1 or 2 ovenproof serving platters, layering with the cheese and jalapeños. Bake until the cheese is melted, 3 to 5 minutes. Remove from the oven and sprinkle with the tomatoes, spring onions, olives and avocados. Serve with salsa on the side.

Layered Fiesta Dip

Makes about 10 to 12 servings

This hearty dip is made of layers of beans, soured cream, salsas, cheese and garnishes. I like to use a variety of salsas for a range of flavours – perhaps Roast Jalapeño Salsa (page 16) or Chipotle Salsa (page 34) with the beans, and a tomato-based salsa in the soured cream. Avoid salsas made with uncooked tomatoes, as the liquid from the tomatoes will pool in the soured cream. Serve with corn chips and raw vegetables.

INGREDIENTS

250 g/9 oz refried beans
75 g/3 oz salsa of your choice
350 ml/12 fl oz soured cream
75 g/3 oz second salsa of your choice
250 g/9 oz Avocado Salsa (page 22)
275 g/10 oz grated Cheddar cheese
75 g/3 oz chopped spring onions
50 g/2 oz sliced black olives, well-drained
1 avocado, peeled, stoned and diced

56

METHOD

▶ Preheat the oven to 180°C/350°F/Gas Mark 4. Mix the beans with the first salsa, spread this mixture on a large ovenproof platter, and sprinkle the Cheddar cheese evenly across the top. Put in the oven until the beans are hot and the cheese has melted, about 10 minutes.

▶ While the beans are heating, mix the soured cream with the second salsa. Remove the beans from the oven and spread the soured cream and salsa mixture on top, then the Avocado Salsa. Finally sprinkle the Cheddar cheese over the top. Garnish with the spring onions, olives and avocado.

Sorting green chillies into bags for sale.

Seafood Salsa Spread

Makes 4 to 6 servings

This simple spread is made by combining salsa and seafood, then pouring it over a block of cream cheese. Use a tomato-based salsa of your choice, but it should be a cooked salsa or one made with grilled tomatoes, as raw tomatoes will exude watery juice. Serve with biscuits or raw vegetables.

INGREDIENTS

175 g/6 oz tomato-based salsa
about 75 g/3 oz tiny cooked prawns or crabmeat
225 g/8 oz cream cheese

METHOD

▶ Mix the salsa and prawns or crabmeat. Place the cream cheese on a serving dish and pour the salsa over the top.

Homemade Tortilla Chips

Makes 4 to 6 servings

Sometimes, nothing but warm tortilla chips will do with homemade salsas. Fortunately they are not difficult to make. However, unless you have two large frying pans, you'll be able to fry only a few tortilla chips at a time.

INGREDIENTS

12 stale tortillas
100 g/4 oz salt (optional)
oil for frying

METHOD

► To make the chips, cut stale tortillas into strips or wedges. (If the tortillas are fresh, dry them slightly by spreading them out and letting them sit for an hour or so.) If you want salted chips, make a brine of 100 g/4 oz salt and 475 ml/16 fl oz of water. Briefly dip the tortilla pieces into the brine, then shake off the excess water.

► Pour 1 cm/½ in of vegetable oil into a large frying pan and heat until the oil is hot but not smoking. Add the chips. If they are wet with brine, take care because the oil will splatter. Cook the chips until golden, turning once or

twice, about 3 minutes, depending on how hot the oil is. Remove the chips from the oil, holding them briefly over the pan to drain off excess oil, then place them on paper towels to drain thoroughly. Give the oil a few moments to reheat, then add a new batch of chips.

► A fat-free cooking alternative is to bake the chips. Preheat the oven to 160°C/325°F/Gas Mark 3. Spread the prepared tortillas in a single layer on an ungreased baking sheet. Bake, turning occasionally, until they are crisp and lightly browned, about 40 minutes.

Empanadas

Makes about 30

Empanadas are little Mexican meat pies, baked or fried. Traditional empanadas may have a crust made of masa harina, the ground corn used for making tortillas and tamales, while some modern interpretations use envelopes of filo pastry. This recipe uses a shortcrust pastry to enclose a spicy-sweet meat filling flavoured with salsa.

INGREDIENTS FOR THE CRUST

350 g/12 oz plain flour
1¹/₂ tsp salt
175 g/7 oz lard or solid shortening
6 tbsp cold water

METHOD

▶ Mix together the flour and salt, then cut in the fat with 2 sharp knives, a pastry cutter, or in a food processor, until the mixture resembles fine crumbs. Stir in the water. If using a food processor, do this step by hand so you can feel the moisture in the dough. The dough should form a moist ball. If it is too crumbly, add 1 tsp water at a time until it is moist but not sticky. Refrigerate for at least 1 hour, then remove and let it return to room temperature, approximately 1 hour, before rolling.

▶ Pinch off about half the dough. Roll out on a floured board to a thickness of 3 mm/¹/₈ inch or less. Cut out 7.5-cm/3-inch circles, then gather up the scraps, add to the rest of the dough, and roll out another batch. This should be enough dough for about 30 empanadas.

INGREDIENTS FOR THE SAVOURY MEAT FILLING

450 g/1 lb lean ground beef
75 g/3 oz chopped onion
350 g/12 oz Salsa Cruda (pages 18–19),
  drained of excess liquid
40 g/1¹/₂ oz toasted slivered almonds,
  coarsely chopped (see Note 1 below)
50 g/2 oz raisins
¹/₂ tsp ground cumin
¹/₂ tsp ground cloves
1 tsp salt
¹/₄ tsp pepper

METHOD

▶ Sauté the ground beef and onion in a hot frying pan until the meat is browned, about 6 to 8 minutes. Add the salsa and cook for about 5 minutes to get rid of any excess liquid. Add the remaining ingredients, mix well and cook for 2 minutes longer.

▶ Place a spoonful of filling in the centre of each circle of pastry. Fold over the pastry and seal the edges so it forms a crescent.

▶ Empanadas can be glazed (see Note 2 below) and baked until golden in a 200°C/400°F/Gas Mark 6 oven, about 15 minutes. Or they can be deep-fried in oil at 190°C/375°F until golden brown, 1 to 2 minutes a side. If you fry them, make sure the edges are well sealed so the filling doesn't leak out.

Note 1: To toast almonds, spread them in a single layer on a small baking sheet. Bake in a 180°C/350°F/Gas Mark 4 oven for 8 to 10 minutes, until golden brown.

Note 2: To make a glaze, with a fork lightly beat 2 eggs with 3 tbsp milk or cream. Brush the glaze over the empanadas before baking.

60

Chilli con Queso

Makes 4 to 6 servings

This hot cheese dip seasoned with roast chillies is popular in Texas and New Mexico. It is served bubbling hot from the oven with tortilla chips. Since it is a dense mixture, use thick chips, not thin ones that crumble easily. You can use leftover Roast Jalapeño Salsa (page 16), or make the simpler roast chilli salsa below.

INGREDIENTS

225 g/8 oz grated Cheddar cheese
100 g/4 oz Roast Jalapeño Salsa (page 16)

METHOD

► Preheat the oven to 180°C/350°F/Gas Mark 4. Mix the cheese and salsa in an ovenproof serving dish and bake until the cheese is bubbling, about 10 minutes. Serve immediately.

► As an alternative, make a simple salsa by roasting about 8 jalapeño chillies until the skins blister and turn brown. Put roast jalapeños in a bag for 10 minutes so steam will loosen the skins. Scrape the skins off the chillies, then remove the stems. Cut in half lengthwise and remove seeds and veins. Finely chop the jalapeños and mix with 1 minced clove garlic and 2 tbsp minced spring onion.

62

Tostaditas

Makes 6 to 8 servings

Tostaditas, or little tostadas, make great finger food. Start with round tortilla chips as a base and build individual appetizers. Use shredded beef or chicken, or refried beans, then add cheese, olives, avocados, salsa, spring onions, sliced jalapeños, or any other toppings you like. Assemble them in advance for guests (but not too far in advance, since you don't want them to get soggy) or lay out the toppings and let them build their own. Below are some suggestions.

INGREDIENTS

10–12 oz/275–300 g bag tortilla chips

One or more of the following:
Chorizo-Bean Dip (page 53)
Shredded beef mixed with Red Chilli Sauce (page 33)
cooked whole prawns
shredded chicken

One or two kinds of cheese:
Something traditional like Cheddar or Lancashire, and a more unusual choice, such as goat's cheese or Roquefort

Two kinds of salsa:
A traditional dipping salsa, and a less predictable choice, such as Chipotle Salsa (page 34) or Sweet Red Pepper Salsa (page 20)

Use a selection of the following garnishes:
One or two kinds of olives
Strips of roasted sweet red pepper or poblanos
Rings of fresh or pickled jalapeño chillies
Chopped spring onions
Diced avocado
Sprigs of coriander

METHOD

▶ Layer the desired toppings on each corn chip and eat.

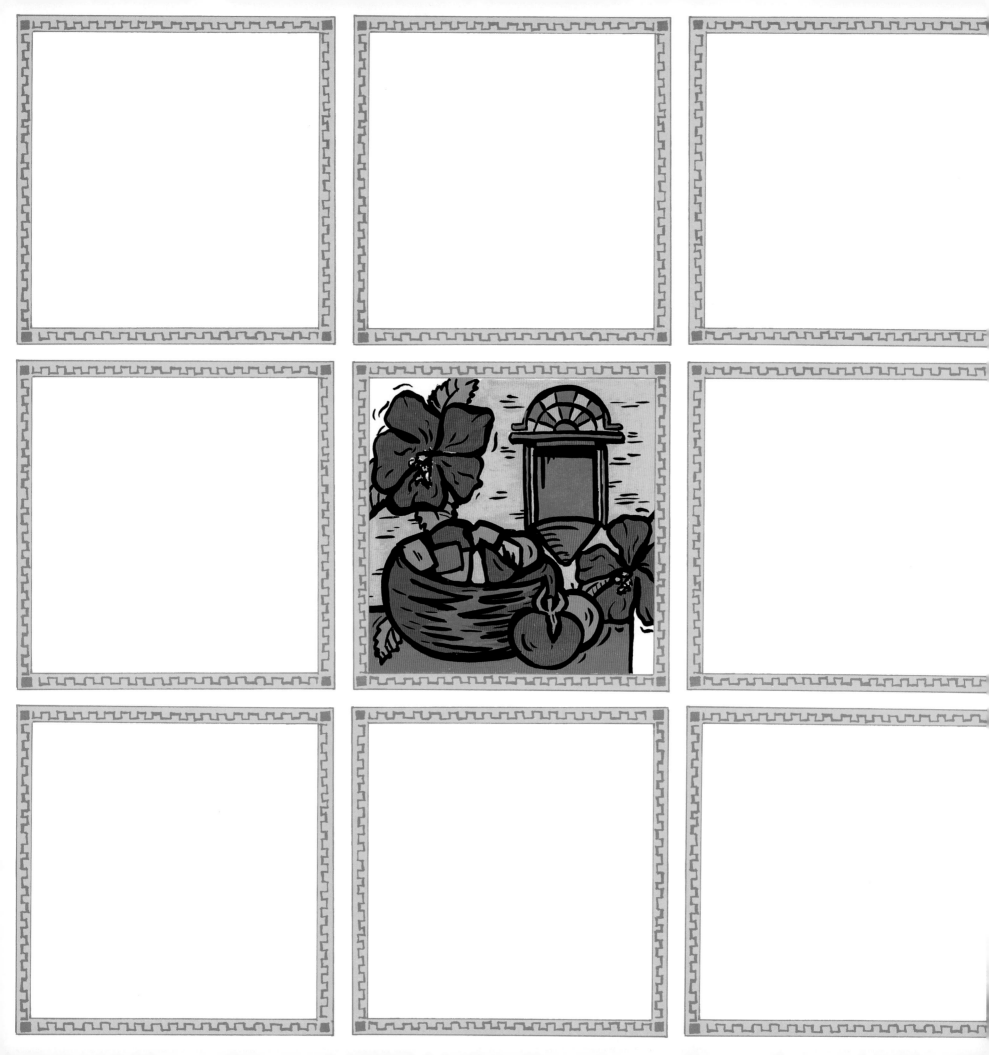

salads

Avocado-Prawn Boats
Salmon Salad with Black
Bean-Papaya Salsa
Tomato Salad with Olive Salsa
Sweetcorn Salsa Salad
with Avocados
Black-eyed Bean Salad
Fajita Salad
Jicama-Orange Salad
Chicken-Rice Salad

Avocado-Prawn Boats

Makes 4 servings

In this salad, spicy fruit salsa is combined with the cool, mellow flavour of perfectly ripe avocado. It makes an excellent first course. Try fresh crab as a substitute for the tiny prawns. You can make the salsa and mix in the prawns in advance, but don't cut the avocados until just before serving as they tend to brown quickly.

INGREDIENTS

100 g/4 oz cooked prawns
175 g/6 oz Mango Salsa (page 46) or
Nectarine Salsa (page 45)
2 ripe but firm avocados

METHOD

▶ Mix the prawns with the salsa. Cut the avocados in half and scoop out the stones. Mound the salsa into the avocado halves. If absolutely necessary, scoop out a little of the avocado flesh to make room for the salsa.

Salmon Salad
with Black Bean-Papaya Salsa

Makes 4 servings

This simple salad is topped with an exotic salsa rather than salad dressing, for an exciting and unusual combination.

INGREDIENTS

300 g/11 oz mixed green salad
350–450 g/12 oz–1 lb Barbecued Salmon
    (page 122), chilled
350 g/12 oz Black Bean-Papaya Salsa
    (page 46)

METHOD

▶ Clean and tear the salad leaves and divide them among 4 plates. Break the salmon into chunks, removing any bones. Divide the salmon among the plates. Top each salad with 75 g/3 oz Black Bean-Papaya Salsa.

Tomato Salad with Olive Salsa

Makes 4 servings

This simple salad depends on excellent ingredients – perfectly ripe tomatoes, fresh (not pre-packed) mozzarella cheese, and fresh basil leaves. Top it with Olive Salsa for a luscious summer dish.

INGREDIENTS

4 large, ripe tomatoes
several sprigs of fresh basil
100 g/4 oz fresh mozzarella cheese
about 175 g/6 oz Olive Salsa (page 22)

METHOD

▶ Core the tomatoes and cut them into thick slices. Arrange the slices on 4 salad plates. Rinse the basil, pull off the leaves and dry them between paper towels. Arrange the basil leaves on top of the tomato slices. Cut the mozzarella into thin slices and place on top of the tomato and basil. Spoon the olive salsa over the tomatoes and cheese.

68

Tomatoes for sale in a market in Mexico.

Sweetcorn Salsa Salad with Avocados

70

Makes 8 servings

This pretty, crunchy salad is an excellent dish for a picnic or barbecue. It can be made early in the day except for the avocados, which should be added at the last minute.

INGREDIENTS

800 g/1¾ lb Sweetcorn Salsa (page 21)
250 g/9 oz cooked sweetcorn
425 g/15 oz can kidney beans, rinsed and drained
1 small, thin courgette, thinly sliced
3 cloves garlic, minced
2 tbsp chopped fresh coriander
¼ tsp ground cumin
2 ripe avocados, peeled, stoned and cubed

METHOD

▶ Mix the Sweetcorn Salsa with the sweetcorn, kidney beans, courgette, garlic, coriander, and cumin. Add the avocado just before serving, and stir in well so it is thoroughly coated with the salsa. Taste and adjust the seasoning.

Black-eyed Bean Salad

Makes 8 servings

This zesty side dish is well suited to a picnic or barbecue. It is best when very spicy, so be sure to make the salsa with jalapeño seeds, or add an extra jalapeño with seeds. The black-eyed beans have a pleasantly nutty flavour, but you can substitute other beans, such as haricot beans. This recipe uses canned beans, but if you have time to soak and cook dried beans, it will improve the flavour. Make the salad several hours in advance, but no more than 12 hours or it will start to lose its crunchy texture.

INGREDIENTS

3 450-g/1/lb cans cooked black-eyed beans, rinsed and drained
675 g/1½ lb Salsa Cruda III (page 19), made with an additional jalapeño if desired
2 tbsp red wine vinegar
2 tbsp olive oil
salt and pepper to taste

METHOD

▶ Combine all the ingredients. Refrigerate for at least 2 hours before serving.

71

Fajita Salad

Makes 4 servings

Crisp lettuce is topped with fajita meat, avocado, and raw vegetables, then served with a spicy salsa instead of a traditional dressing. It is a great way to use leftovers from a fajita party. Use Barbecued Chicken (page 110), Salsa-marinated Flank Steak (page 109), or beef barbecued for Fajitas (page 98).

INGREDIENTS

300 g/11 oz cos or other lettuce
350 g/12 oz cold grilled meat, cut into thin
 strips
1 avocado, peeled, stoned and diced
several thin slices of red onion, separated
 into rings
several radishes, thinly sliced
1 small sweet pepper, cut into strips
200 g/7 oz tomato-based salsa

METHOD

▶ Divide the lettuce among 4 large plates. Top with the meat, avocado, onion, radishes and sweet pepper. Serve the salsa on the side.

Jicama-Orange Salad

Makes 4 to 6 servings

This refreshing salad combines the crunch of fresh jicama, the tang of oranges, the bite of onion and the heat of jalapeño chilli. It is served with a slightly sweet dressing for an unusual flavour.

INGREDIENTS

3 medium oranges
1/2 medium red onion
175 g/6 oz peeled jicama, cut into 1-cm/1/2-in
 cubes
dressing (recipe follows)
lettuce leaves

METHOD

▶ Peel the oranges and slice them thinly, removing the pips. Thinly slice the onion, then separate the slices into rings. Mix the orange, onion and jicama together, toss with the dressing, and serve over lettuce.

DRESSING

6 tbsp olive oil
3 tbsp red wine vinegar
2 tbsp orange juice
2 tsp honey
1/4 tsp chilli powder
1 jalapeño chilli, unseeded, finely chopped

METHOD

▶ Combine all the ingredients in a bottle and shake well to mix.

Chicken-Rice Salad

Makes 4 to 6 servings

Serve this salad on a bed of lettuce for a delicious luncheon dish. It is best when the chicken is marinated and grilled, as for Barbecued Chicken (page 110), but any cooked chicken will do.

INGREDIENTS

575 g/1¼ lb cooked white rice
2 chicken breast halves, cooked and cubed
250 g/9 oz Salsa Cruda III (page 19)
25 g/1 oz chopped spring onions
40 g/1½ oz toasted slivered almonds (see right)
1 avocado, peeled, stoned and diced
1 tbsp red wine vinegar
salt to taste

METHOD

► Combine all the ingredients. Taste and adjust the seasonings.

To toast almonds: Spread them in a single layer on a small baking sheet. Bake at 180°C/350°F/Gas Mark 4 until golden brown, 7 to 10 minutes.

73

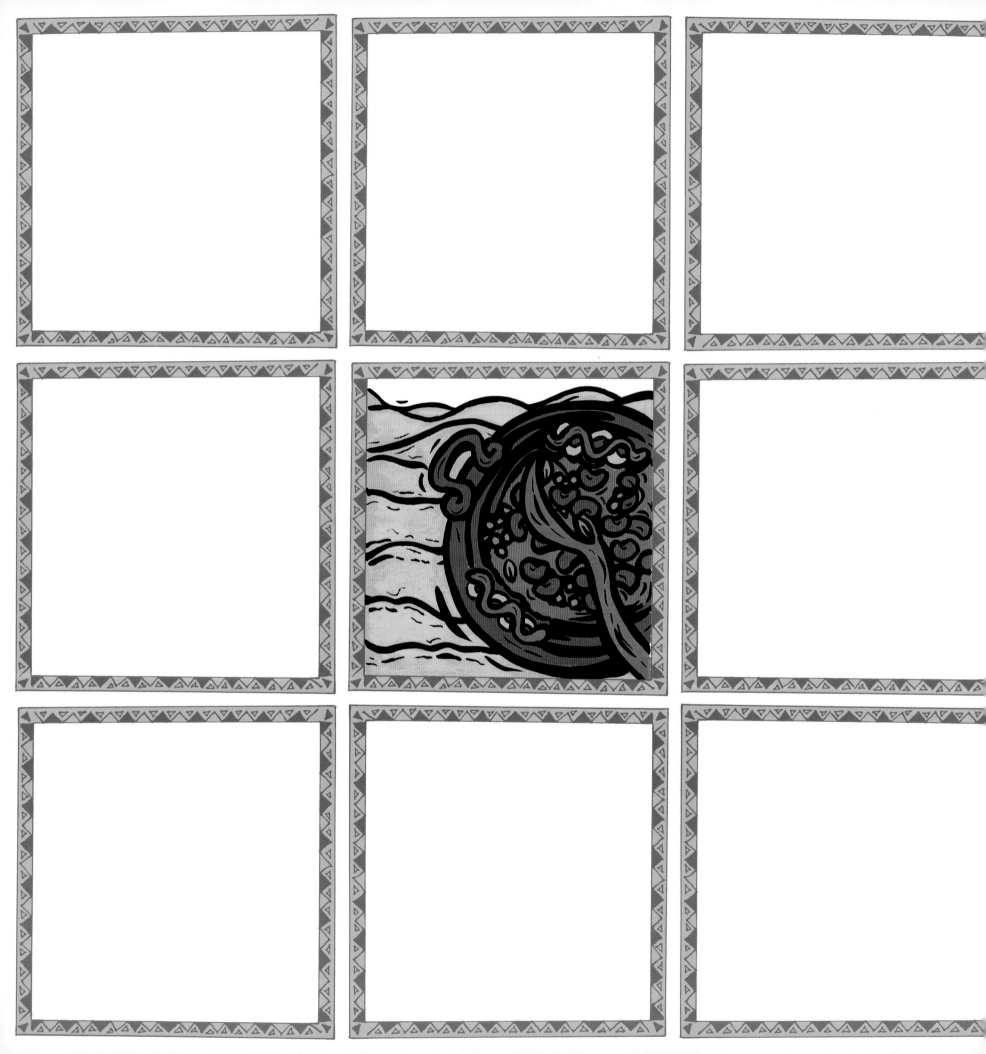

soups, stews and bean dishes

Avocado Soup
Tomato-Basil Soup with
Sweet Red Pepper Salsa
Lime-Tortilla Soup
Spicy Crab-Corn Chowder
Black Bean Soup with Chorizo
Pozole

Barbecued Seafood Soup
Red Beans and Rice
Feijoada

Avocado Soup

Makes 4 servings

This easy, no-cook soup is wonderful on a summer day, when avocados are plentiful and cheap. Be sure that the avocados are perfectly ripe, but not overripe, since this soup shows off their flavour. Serve it cold, garnished with a crunchy salsa. Although the soup needs to be made at least 2 hours in advance, it does not keep well if made more than 8 hours in advance.

INGREDIENTS

3 ripe avocados, peeled and stoned
300 ml/½ pint chicken stock
250 ml/8 fl oz single cream
1 tsp salt
¼ tsp cayenne
175 g/6 oz Cucumber Salsa (page 20) or Salsa
  Cruda III (page 19)

METHOD

▶ Put all the ingredients except the salsa in a blender or food processor and purée until smooth. Chill for at least 2 hours. Stir well to blend in any darkening on the surface and serve, garnished with the salsa.

Tomato-Basil Soup
with Sweet Red Pepper Salsa

77

Makes 4 servings

This is a delightful hot-weather soup, perfect for late summer when the garden is producing an abundance of tomatoes. Don't use hard, pink, pre-packed tomatoes, since this recipe relies on the lush flavour of ripe tomatoes. The soup should be made early in the day, then chilled until serving time. For a slightly spicier flavour, substitute Roast Jalapeño Salsa (page 16) for the Sweet Red Pepper Salsa.

INGREDIENTS

2 cloves garlic, minced
5 tbsp chopped fresh basil
¼ tsp freshly ground black pepper
3 tbsp extra-virgin olive oil
1.75 kg/4 lb ripe tomatoes

250 ml/8 fl oz chicken stock
1 tbsp balsamic vinegar
½ tsp salt
about 75 g/3 oz Sweet Red Pepper Salsa
(page 20)

METHOD

▶ In a small bowl, mix together the garlic, 1 tbsp basil, the black pepper and olive oil. Lightly crush the garlic with the back of a spoon to release the juices into the oil. Let the mixture steep while you prepare the tomatoes.

▶ Peel the tomatoes by dropping them into a pan of boiling water for about 40 seconds. Let them cool slightly, then slip off the skins. Cut

them in half and squeeze out the seeds. Core and coarsely chop the tomatoes.

▶ Put the tomatoes, chicken stock, and garlic-oil mixture into a medium saucepan. Bring to the boil, then reduce the heat to low and simmer, uncovered, for 1 hour. Add the remaining basil, the balsamic vinegar and salt, then purée the soup. Taste and adjust the seasonings. Chill until serving time.

▶ Top each bowl of soup with 1 to 2 tablespoons Sweet Red Pepper Salsa, which should be stirred into the soup.

Lime-Tortilla Soup

Makes 4 main-course servings

This is a variation on a traditional Mexican soup – chicken stock flavoured with salsa and lime, poured over tortilla chips and shredded chicken, then garnished with cheese. Make sure you include some jalapeño seeds when you make the salsa, or the soup will be only mildly spicy. Ideally the chicken should be marinated in lime juice, olive oil and garlic, then barbecued, but boiled, poached or roast chicken are fine too. You can use bought tortilla chips, but it's even better when you make your own by frying strips of tortilla in hot oil.

INGREDIENTS

250 g/9 oz Salsa Cruda I (page 18)
1 litre/1¾ pints chicken stock
2 tortillas
2–3 tbsp vegetable oil
2 chicken breast halves, cooked and shredded
2 tbsp fresh lime juice
salt to taste
grated Cheddar cheese or dry Mexican cheese, for garnish

METHOD

▶ Cut the tortillas into chip-size strips. Heat the oil in a frying pan until it is very hot but not smoking. Quickly fry the tortilla strips in batches until they are crisp, 1 to 2 minutes a side. Drain on paper towels.

▶ Put the salsa and chicken stock in a large saucepan. Bring to the boil, reduce the heat and simmer, covered, for 15 minutes. Meanwhile, divide the tortilla chips and shredded chicken between 4 soup bowls.

▶ In a blender or food processor, purée the soup in batches. Return the soup to the hob and add the lime and salt to taste. Simmer for about 2 minutes longer for flavours to blend. Pour into the soup bowls, sprinkle cheese on top, and serve immediately.

78

Spicy Crab-Corn Chowder

Makes 6 servings

In this delicious crab soup, Roast Sweetcorn Salsa is cooked with chicken stock, cream and crabmeat for a smoky, chunky, slightly spicy cream soup. You will fall instantly in love with it. Use fresh crab rather than canned – you'll be able to taste the difference. If you prefer a spicier soup, leave some of the seeds in the jalapeño when you make the salsa, or add another jalapeño and seeds to the soup.

INGREDIENTS

2 tbsp butter
75 g/3 oz chopped onion
750 ml/1¼ pints chicken stock
575 g/1¼ lb Roast Sweetcorn Salsa (page 29)
250 ml/8 fl oz double cream
½ tsp salt
¼ tsp white pepper
250 ml/8 fl oz soured cream
225 g/8 oz fresh cooked crabmeat
1 tbsp chopped fresh coriander
2 spring onions, chopped

METHOD

▶ Melt the butter in a large, heavy saucepan. Sauté the onion for 5 minutes or until tender. Add the chicken stock and Roast Sweetcorn Salsa. Bring the soup to the boil, then lower the heat, place a lid on the pan slightly askew, and simmer for 20 minutes.

▶ Add the double cream, salt and white pepper, and return to the boil, then whisk in the soured cream and crabmeat. Heat just a couple minutes to warm the soured cream and crab, but don't bring it to the boil as it may curdle. Ladle the soup into bowls and garnish with the coriander and spring onion.

Black Bean Soup with Chorizo

Makes 6 servings

This soup is full of flavour even before you top it with salsa. Some of the spiciness comes from the chorizo sausage, but since chorizo can vary widely, you will need to taste the soup and adjust the seasoning to taste, adding some ground cumin if necessary. Purée the soup if you prefer it smooth.

INGREDIENTS

350 g/12 oz dried black beans
1.25 litres/2¼ pints chicken stock
2 large tomatoes, seeded and chopped
1 tbsp red wine vinegar
2 ancho chillies
450 g/1 lb chorizo sausage
250 g/9 oz chopped onion
2 stalks celery, diced
3 cloves garlic, minced
2–3 tsp salt
½ tsp pepper
½–2 tsp ground cumin (optional)
200 g/7 oz Salsa Cruda I or III (pages 18–19)
soured cream (optional), for garnish

METHOD

▶ Pick over the beans, removing any pebbles, then put them in a large saucepan with 1.25 litres/2¼ pints water. Bring to the boil, boil for 2 minutes, then cover and turn off the heat. Let stand for 1 hour. Drain and rinse the beans, and put them back in the pan with the chicken stock, 750 ml/1¼ pints of water, the chopped tomatoes and the vinegar. Bring to the boil, reduce the heat, and simmer, uncovered, until the beans are tender and the excess liquid has been absorbed, about 1 to 1½ hours.

▶ Meanwhile, prepare the ancho chillies. Cut them in half, remove the stems and some of the seeds. Put them in a small, heat-resistant bowl. Pour 6 tbsp boiling water over the anchos and let them soak for 30 minutes, stirring once or twice to be sure all of them are soaking. Drain and discard the water. Put the anchos and 6 tbsp of fresh water into a blender or food processor and purée. Add the purée to the beans.

▶ Next, prepare the chorizo and vegetables. Remove the sausage skin and crumble the meat into a frying pan. Fry until the excess fat has cooked out. Tilt the pan to drain the sausage, remove the sausage with a slotted spoon and add to the beans.

▶ Discard all but 1 tbsp of chorizo fat. Add the onion and celery to the fat and sauté for 5 minutes. Add the garlic and sauté for 1 minute longer. Add the vegetables to the beans.

▶ When the beans are tender, taste and add salt, pepper, and cumin if needed. Simmer for 2 minutes longer to allow the flavours to blend. If desired, purée the soup in batches. (The soup can be made in advance to this point and refrigerated.) Return the soup to the pan and briefly reheat it. Ladle into soup bowls and garnish with salsa and with soured cream, if desired.

Pozole

Makes 8 main-course servings

Pozole, a long-simmering pork and hominy stew, is a traditional dish that dates back many centuries with Mexicans and American Indians of the South West. Historically, it is made with dried hominy and the stock is often cooked with pigs' feet. However, dried hominy is not readily available, and some people are squeamish about using pigs' feet. For those reasons, and as a shortcut, this recipe uses canned hominy and neck bones instead. Other pork bones may be used too. This version of pozole is a main dish, but you can omit the cubed pork and serve it as a side dish or first course, if you prefer. Serve with Cucumber Salsa or Salsa Cruda II, to be spooned over the stew.

INGREDIENTS

115 g/4¹/₂ oz chopped onion
4 tbsp vegetable oil
3 cloves garlic, minced
1.75 litres/3 pints chicken stock
450 g/1 lb pork neck bones
2 ancho chillies
2 dried California chillies
3 tbsp flour
1 tsp salt
1 tsp dried mustard
2 tsp dried oregano
2 tsp ground cumin
¹/₂ tsp cayenne
¹/₂ tsp black pepper
1.5 kg/3 lb pork loin or other pork cut, cut into bite-sized cubes
675 g/1¹/₂ lb canned hominy
450 g/1 lb Cucumber Salsa (page 20) or Salsa Cruda II (page 18)

METHOD

► In a large stockpot, sauté the onion in 1 tbsp oil for 5 minutes. Add the garlic and cook for 1 minute longer, then add the chicken stock and neck bones. Note the level of the liquid, then add 475 ml/16 fl oz water. If the stock falls below that level during cooking, add more water. Bring the stew to the boil, reduce the heat, and simmer, uncovered, for 2 hours.

► While the stew is simmering, cut the dried chillies in half and remove the seeds. Put the chillies in a small, heat-resistant bowl and pour 6 tbsp boiling water over them. Let soak for 20 minutes, stirring once or twice to be sure all parts of chillies are softened. Purée the water and chillies in a blender, then add this purée to the simmering stew.

► After the stew has simmered for 2 hours, remove it from the heat. Remove the pork bones. If you have time, let the stock and the bones cool for ease of handling. Skim the fat from the stock and return the stock to the hob. Take off any meat from the bones and add it to the stew. Discard the bones and fat.

► Mix together the flour, salt, mustard, oregano, cumin, cayenne and black pepper. Toss the pork cubes in this seasoning mixture until evenly coated. Heat the remaining oil in a large frying pan and sauté the pork just until it is golden brown. Add the pork cubes to the stew, bring to the boil, then reduce the heat and simmer, covered, for 20 minutes. Add the hominy and simmer for 10 minutes longer.

► Taste the stock and adjust the salt to taste. Ladle the pozole into large bowls and serve with Cucumber Salsa or Salsa Cruda II.

81

Ocotlán market in Mexico.

Barbecued Seafood Soup

Makes 4 servings

The flavours of barbecued seafood and salsa combine for a spicy soup that is low in fat. This recipe calls for prawns and scallops, but you can substitute other barbecued seafood or fish. The size is not important (tiny prawns are not recommended), although smaller pieces may fall through the grid. You can also substitute a different salsa – any smooth, tomato-based one is good. Since the spiciness of the soup depends on the salsa, a fairly hot one is recommended.

INGREDIENTS

350 g/12 oz prawns, peeled and deveined
350 g/12 oz scallops
3 tbsp olive oil
3 tbsp fresh lime juice
3 cloves garlic, minced
1 tbsp vegetable oil
300 g/11 oz Basic Cooked Salsa (page 32)

1.5 litres/2 pints clam juice or seafood stock
1 tbsp fresh basil or 1 tsp dried
1 tsp fresh thyme or ¼ tsp dried
3 thick slices of onion, separated into rings
½ sweet pepper, cut into chunks
1 or 2 jalapeño chillies, thinly sliced into rounds
salt and pepper to taste

METHOD

▶ Put the seafood in a non-metallic bowl. Mix the olive oil, lime juice and garlic together, pour over the seafood, and stir so all the pieces are coated. Refrigerate the seafood while you prepare the barbecue. It will be easier to cook the seafood if it is threaded on skewers (wooden skewers should be soaked in water for 30 minutes to prevent burning) or if you use a special tray for cooking small items.

▶ Mound coals in the barbecue and let burn until the flames have died and the coals are glowing, 30 to 40 minutes. Spread the coals out. Put the seafood on the oiled grid or tray and cook for 2 to 3 minutes a side. It does not have to be thoroughly cooked since it can finish cooking in the soup, but it should pick up colour and flavour. If the pieces are large, cut into bite-sized chunks.

▶ Heat the vegetable oil in a large saucepan. Add the salsa and fry it for 5 minutes. Add the clam juice or seafood stock and the herbs. Bring to the boil, reduce the heat and simmer, with the lid slightly askew, for 15 minutes. Remove the cover and add the onion, sweet pepper and jalapeño. Simmer for 3 to 4 minutes longer. Add the seafood and cook for 1 to 2 minutes. Add salt and pepper to taste.

8 2

A selection of fresh fish.

Red Beans and Rice

Makes 6 to 8 servings

From Central America to the Caribbean to New Orleans, slow-cooked and highly seasoned red beans and rice is a traditional dish. This main-course version uses leftover pork, but it's good with chunks of sausage or shreds of barbecued beef brisket too. Top with uncooked salsa for colour, crunch and flavour.

INGREDIENTS

350 g/12 oz dried kidney beans
2–3 tbsp vegetable oil
175 g/6 oz chopped onion
2 stalks celery, chopped
3 cloves garlic, minced
275 g/10 oz cooked pork (diced ham, slivers of ham hocks, shredded barbecued or roast pork)

2 bay leaves
1 tsp ground cumin
½ tsp pepper
1–2 tsp salt
800 g/1¾ lb cooked rice
330 g/12 oz Salsa Cruda I (page 18) or Salsa Cruda III (page 19)
soured cream (optional)

METHOD

▶ Pick through the beans for pebbles or other debris. Put the beans in a large saucepan, add water and soak overnight. Or you can bring the beans and water to the boil, boil for 2 minutes, then cover, turn off the heat, and let the beans stand for an hour.

▶ Drain and rinse the beans and put them back in the pan. Add enough water to cover the beans by about 5 cm/2 in, then bring to the boil. Meanwhile prepare the vegetables. Heat the oil in a frying pan. Add the onion and celery and cook for 5 minutes, then add the garlic and cook for 2 minutes longer. Add the vegetables to the beans, along with the pork, bay leaves, cumin and pepper. Reduce the heat and simmer until the beans are tender, 1 to 1½ hours. Check periodically and add more water if needed. Taste and add salt.

▶ Serve the beans over rice, topped with the salsa and with soured cream if desired.

84

Feijoada

Makes 6 to 8 servings

Feijoada is a Brazilian stew of pork and black beans, traditionally eaten with rice and greens. Linguica, a hot Portuguese sausage, gives it its kick.

INGREDIENTS

350 g/12 oz dried black beans
450 g/1 lb pork loin, cut into 2-cm/³/₄-in cubes
salt and pepper to taste
350 g/12 oz Garlic Salsa (page 35)
2 tbsp fresh lemon juice
4 tbsp olive oil
450 g/1 lb linguica sausage, cut into 1-cm/ ¹/₂-in slices

METHOD

▶ Pick through the beans for pebbles or other debris. Put the beans in a large saucepan with 1.75 litres/3 pints water. Let soak overnight, or bring the water to the boil, boil for 2 minutes, then remove from the heat, cover, and let soak for 1 hour.

▶ Put the pork in a non-metallic bowl and sprinkle with salt and pepper. Combine half the Garlic Salsa with the lemon juice and 2 tbsp olive oil, mix with the pork, and let it marinate for about 30 minutes. Drain the salsa, but do not discard. Heat the remaining oil in a large frying pan and add the pork. Cook until the cubes are lightly browned, 6 to 8 minutes. They do not have to be cooked thoroughly.

▶ Drain and rinse the beans. Put them in a large stewpot and add enough water to cover the beans by 2.5 cm/1 in. Bring to the boil, then reduce the heat and simmer, uncovered. Check the beans occasionally and add a little more water if needed.

▶ Add the pork, the salsa that was used for marinade, and the remaining salsa to the beans, together with the linguica. Cook until the beans are tender, and the liquid has reduced to a thick sauce, 1 to 1½ hours. Taste and add more salt if necessary. Ladle into bowls and serve.

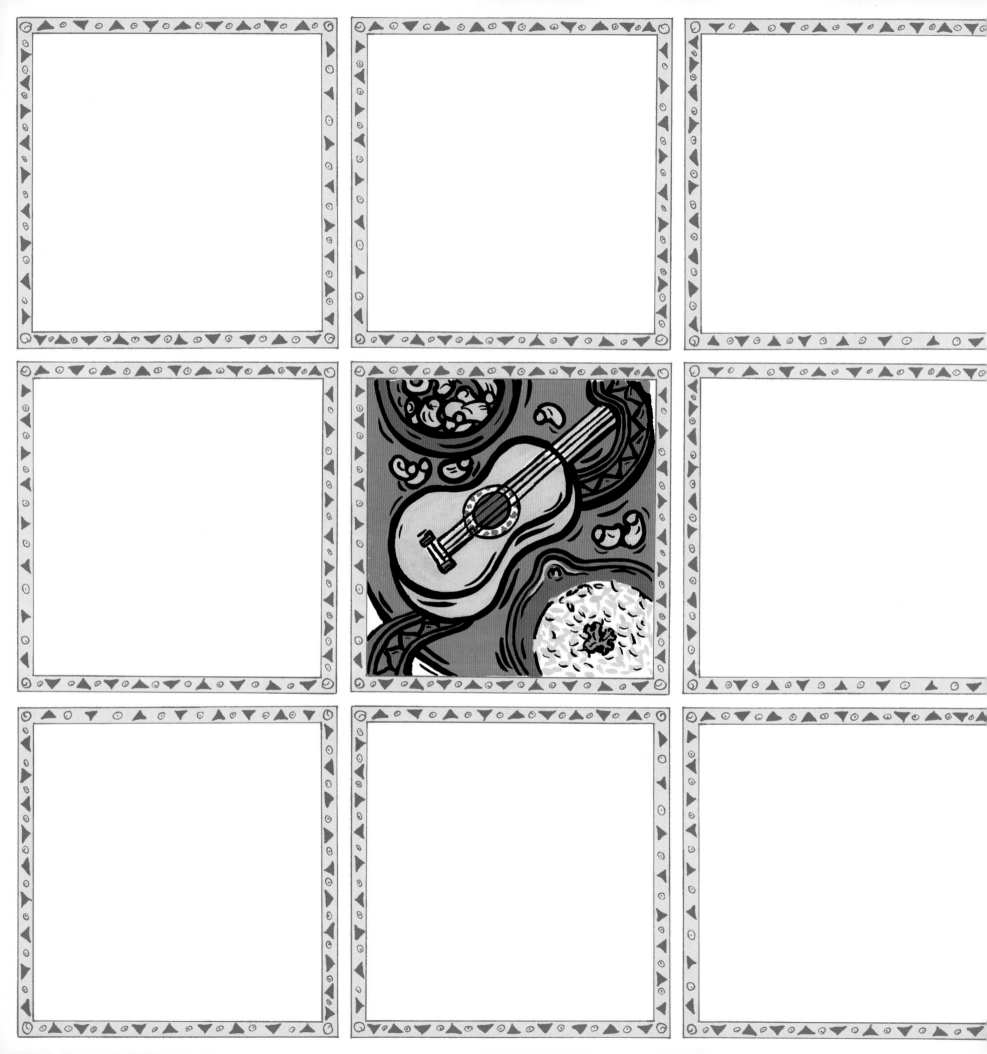

rice, pasta and side dishes

Pasta with Sun-dried Tomato Salsa
Sweetcorn Salsa Muffins
Spanish Rice
Fettucine with Prawns and
Chilli-Cream Sauce
Green Rice

Pasta with Sun-dried Tomato Salsa

88

Makes 4 first-course servings

The intense flavours of this powerful salsa may clash in concentrated form. When it is tossed with pasta, however, the flavours meld and become complementary.

INGREDIENTS

3 tbsp olive oil
6 cloves garlic, minced
1 tsp crushed dried chillies
1 sweet red pepper, cored, seeded and cut into quarters
100 g/4 oz sun-dried tomatoes, packed in oil
1 tbsp chopped fresh basil
4 rashers bacon, cooked and crumbled
50 g/2 oz sliced black olives
350–450 g/12 oz–1 lb pasta
grated Parmesan cheese

METHOD

► Heat the oil in a small frying pan over low heat. Add the garlic and the dried chillies. Cook slowly, stirring often and pressing the garlic to release the juices, until the garlic is lightly browned, 5 to 8 minutes. The heat must be very low or the garlic may scorch and turn bitter. Remove from the heat and let soak while you prepare the other ingredients.

► Cook the red pepper skin side down over a barbecue fire or skin side up under a grill until the skin is blackened. Remove from the heat and place it in a plastic bag to steam for 10 minutes. Peel off the skin and chop the red pepper.

► Chop the sun-dried tomatoes and put them into a small bowl with the basil. Add the bacon, garlic-chilli-olive oil mixture, red pepper, and sliced olives. Cook the pasta in plenty of boiling salted water until just tender. Drain well, and then toss with the salsa and Parmesan cheese.

Sweetcorn Salsa Muffins

Makes 12 to 18 muffins

These muffins are made spicy by the addition of Sweetcorn Salsa. Serve them with salads, soups, stews and chillies. The recipe makes 12 large muffins, or about 18 muffins if you about two-thirds fill the cups with batter.

INGREDIENTS

200 g/7 oz cornmeal
50 g/2 oz plain flour
1 tsp salt
2 tsp baking powder
1 tsp bicarbonate of soda
1 tbsp sugar

3 eggs, lightly beaten
75 g/3 oz butter, melted
about 275 ml/9 fl oz buttermilk
350 g/12 oz Sweetcorn Salsa (page 21)

METHOD

▶ Preheat the oven to 220°C/425°F/Gas Mark 7. Lightly grease some muffin tins.

▶ Mix together all the dry ingredients in a large bowl. In a small bowl, mix the eggs, melted butter and 250 ml/8 fl oz buttermilk. Pour the liquids into the dry ingredients and stir until combined. The batter may be a little lumpy as long as there aren't clumps of dry cornmeal. Stir in the salsa and add more buttermilk if needed. The batter should be fairly thick, so that it pours slowly. For large muffins, fill the cups to the rim. For smaller muffins, fill them two-thirds full.

▶ Bake until the tops are lightly browned and a knife inserted in the centre of a muffin comes out clean, about 18 to 24 minutes, depending on size.

89

Spanish Rice

Makes 6 to 8 servings

This is a spicier version of Spanish Rice than is usually served with Mexican food. The spices are briefly fried to develop their flavour, then rice is added and fried. It is then steamed in water and salsa.

Ingredients

3 tbsp vegetable oil
1 tsp chilli powder
½ tsp ground cumin
½ tsp dried oregano
2 cloves garlic, minced
400 g/14 oz white rice
250 g/9 oz Salsa Cruda I (page 18) or Salsa
*   Cruda III (page 19)*
1 tsp salt

90

Method

▶ Heat the oil in a heavy frying pan. Add the chilli powder, cumin, oregano and garlic and cook for 1 minute, stirring constantly. If the oil is very hot, remove the pan from the heat and let the spices cook in the heat from the oil. After 1 minute, add the rice. Cook for 10 minutes, stirring almost constantly.

▶ If the pan is large and deep (at least 1.5-litre/ 2¾-pint capacity), add 600 ml/1 pint water, the salsa and the salt. If it is not large enough, transfer the seasoned rice to a large pan and add the water, salsa and salt. Bring to the boil, cover and reduce the heat. Cook until the liquid has been absorbed and the rice is tender, 20 to 25 minutes. Fluff with a fork. Let stand, covered, for 5 minutes, then serve.

Olvera in the province of Cadiz.

Fettucine with Prawns and Chilli-Cream Sauce

Makes 6 first-course or 4 main-course servings

Here's a spicy variation on Fettucine Alfredo, with Roast Jalapeño Salsa and prawns cooked in the cream sauce. Time this dish so that the fettucine finishes cooking just as the sauce is done. If it finishes a minute or two ahead of the sauce, toss with a scant amount of olive oil.

INGREDIENTS

75 g/3 oz butter
75 g/3 oz Roast Jalapeño Salsa (page 16)
350 g/12 oz medium to large prawns, cleaned
450 g/1 lb fettucine
250 ml/8 fl oz double cream
1/2 tsp salt
pinch of white pepper
50 g/2 oz grated Parmesan cheese, plus extra for garnish

METHOD

► Melt 25 g/1 oz butter in a large frying pan. Add 1 tbsp Roast Jalapeño Salsa and cook for 1 minute, stirring. Add the prawns and sauté until they curl tightly and are an opaque white-pink, 2 to 3 minutes. Remove them with a slotted spoon and set aside.

► Cook the fettucine in plenty of boiling salted water until just tender, then drain. While the pasta is cooking, add the remaining butter to the frying pan in which you cooked the prawns. When it is melted and foamy, add the remaining salsa. Cook, stirring, for 1 minute, then add the cream, salt and white pepper, and cook until the sauce thickens slightly, about 3 minutes. Stir in the prawns, then stir in the Parmesan cheese and the cooked, drained noodles. Toss until the noodles are coated. Serve with additional Parmesan sprinkled on top.

92

Green Rice

Makes 6 to 8 servings

This spicy rice dish is flavoured with coriander and Roast Jalapeño Salsa.

INGREDIENTS

175 g/6 oz Roast Jalapeño Salsa (page 16)
25 g/1 oz fresh coriander
25 g/1 oz fresh parsley
750 ml/1¼ pints chicken stock
3 tbsp vegetable oil
400 g/14 oz white rice
1½ tsp salt

METHOD

▶ In a blender or food processor, purée the salsa, coriander and parsley with about 250 ml/8 fl oz chicken stock. Set aside.

▶ Heat the oil in a frying pan. Add the rice and cook, stirring frequently, 10 minutes. If the pan does not have at least a 1.5-litre/2¾-pint capacity, transfer the rice to a large pan. Add the purée, the remaining stock and the salt to the rice. Bring to the boil, cover and reduce the heat. Cook until the liquid has been absorbed and the rice is tender, 20 to 25 minutes. Fluff the rice with a fork and let stand, covered, for another 5 minutes before serving.

mexican dishes

Quesadillas
Fajitas
Chicken Enchiladas with
Green Chilli Sauce
Beef Enchiladas with
Red Chilli Sauce
Tostadas
Black Bean Chillies Rellenos

Quesadillas

Quesadillas have become ubiquitous, showing up in all kinds of restaurants, Mexican or not, with a variety of fillings – goat's cheese, smoked chicken, lobster, and just about anything else imaginable. True Mexican quesadillas are cheese empanadas – turnovers made with fresh corn tortilla masa. But here we go the easy route, using the popular flour tortilla version.

Quesadillas are typically served with a tomato salsa, but don't overlook the possibilities of a tomatillo salsa, black bean salsa or avocado salsa. Or use two salsas – one type in the filling, and another for dipping. If you're feeling really bold, try a fruit salsa with a meat or fish filling.

The easiest way to cook quesadillas is over a griddle. But since not many people have a griddle, here are instructions for making them in a frying pan.

INGREDIENTS

For each quesadilla, you will need:
vegetable oil or lard
1 flour tortilla
40 g/1¹/₂ oz grated cheese or 2 10-cm/4-in
squares of sliced Cheddar – or any other
type of cheese you prefer

METHOD

▶ Very lightly oil a heavy frying pan that is at least as large as the tortilla (usually about 20 cm/8 in in diameter). You only need enough oil to season the tortilla and keep it from sticking. Heat the pan, then place the tortilla in it, making sure it lies flat. Reduce the heat to low. Place the cheese on one half of the tortilla, and fold the other half over. Lightly brush the top of the folded tortilla with oil. As the cheese begins to melt and the quesadilla holds together, carefully turn it over. Cook until the cheese has completely melted and the tortilla has a few brown spots.

▶ Remove from the heat, cut into wedges, and serve with salsa for dipping.

▶ Instead of folding the tortilla, you can double the amount of cheese and make a sandwich with a second tortilla. This method is faster if you're cooking quesadillas for a large number of people.

▶ For variety, add any combination of the following to the cheese filling:

strips of roast poblano or jalapeño chillies,
or sweet red pepper
chopped spring onions
chopped coriander
mushrooms sautéed in butter and garlic
cooked meat, such as barbecued chicken,
smoked sausage, beef or pork
cooked seafood, such as prawns or crab
Black Bean Salsa (page 26)

▶ The following items are best cold, rather than cooked in the quesadilla, so serve them over the top, or pry open the cooked quesadilla and put them inside:

black olives
sliced avocado
chopped fresh tomatoes
soured cream (on top or as a dip)

Produce under protective awnings in a Mexican market.

Fajitas

98

Makes 4 servings

Fajitas, thinly-sliced barbecued beef wrapped in tortillas and maybe salsa, sprang up in Texas in the 1970s, then swept the United States in the 1980s. The original fajitas used a skirt steak off the diaphragm area of the steer, but many other cuts of beef are commonly used as well. From its simple beginnings, the fajita has become a garnish-laden meal, accompanied by cheese, guacamole and soured cream. This version keeps it simple: marinated barbecued beef, salsa, and some sautéed peppers and onions are wrapped in flour tortillas. For variety, substitute Barbecued Chicken (page 110) or barbecued pork. Another marinade option is the one used in Salsa-marinated Flank Steak (page 109).

INGREDIENTS

675 g/1½ lb skirt or flank steak
350 ml/12 fl oz beer
150 ml/¼ pint olive oil
3 tbsp red wine vinegar
4 cloves garlic, minced
½ tsp salt
¼ tsp pepper
2 green sweet peppers
1 medium onion
2 tbsp vegetable oil
12 flour tortillas
250 g/9 oz salsa of your choice

METHOD

▶ Pierce the beef all over with a fork, then put it in a shallow glass dish. Make a marinade by combining the beer, olive oil, vinegar, garlic, salt and pepper. Pour the marinade over the beef, turning the meat to be sure it is completely coated. Marinate overnight.

▶ About an hour before you plan to eat, light a fire in the barbecue. Cut the peppers into strips. Cut the onion into thick horizontal slices, then separate the rings. Heat the oil in a frying pan, and cook the onion slowly over low heat until golden, about 25 minutes. Add the pepper strips during the last 5 minutes.

▶ When the flames in the barbecue have died and the coals are glowing, put the meat on the grid. Discard the marinade. Cook until the meat is done to your liking. Small skirt steaks will take about 10 to 15 minutes; flank steak will take longer.

▶ While the meat is cooking, warm the tortillas by wrapping them in a damp towel and putting them in a 180°C/350°F/Gas Mark 4 oven for about 10 minutes. Slice the beef thinly, then serve wrapped in tortillas with the sautéed onions and peppers and the salsa.

Chicken Enchiladas with Green Chilli Sauce

Makes 6 servings

These enchiladas are not as spicy as the red ones because the Green Chilli Sauce is mellowed by the addition of soured cream. Sliced fresh avocado makes a good garnish.

INGREDIENTS

175 ml/6 fl oz soured cream
575 g/1¼ lb Green Chilli Sauce (page 32)
oil for frying
12 corn tortillas
375 g/13 oz shredded cooked chicken
450 g/1 lb grated Cheddar cheese

METHOD

▶ Preheat the oven to 180°C/350°F/Gas Mark 4. Have ready a large, shallow baking dish about 33 × 23 cm/13 × 9 in. Stir the soured cream into the Green Chilli Sauce, then pour into a wide, shallow dish.

▶ The process here is to fry the tortillas, dip them in the sauce, fill them with chicken and cheese, roll them, and place them in the baking dish. Set up the utensils and ingredients so you can do this like an assembly line.

▶ Pour oil into a frying pan to a depth of 5 mm/¼ in. Heat until hot, but not smoking, then add the first tortilla. Fry the tortilla just long enough to heat and soften it, 2 to 3 seconds per side. Hold the tortilla just above the pan for a few moments so excess oil can drain off. The heat under the pan should be high enough to reheat the oil after each tortilla, but not so high that it overheats and smokes while you are assembling each enchilada.

▶ Working quickly, dip the tortilla in the sauce so both sides are immersed. It's all right if not very much adheres. Now remove the tortilla and lay it flat. Spread 3 tbsp shredded chicken in a thin line up the centre of the tortilla and sprinkle 2 to 3 tbsp grated cheese over it. If the tortilla does not have much green sauce on it, dab a little over the filling. Tightly roll the enchilada into a cylinder and put it, seam-side down, in the baking-dish.

▶ Repeat the process until you have used up the tortillas and chicken, squeezing the enchiladas into a single layer in the baking dish, if possible.

▶ Spoon the remaining sauce over the enchiladas, then sprinkle over the remaining cheese. Bake, uncovered, for 15 minutes. Serve immediately.

99

Beef Enchiladas with Red Chilli Sauce

Makes 6 servings

Enchiladas, one of Mexico's most popular dishes, are a combination of meat, cheese and sauce rolled up in a soft tortilla and baked. I like to use barbecued meat – such as leftover Salsa-marinated Flank Steak (page 108) – because it gives them extra flavour, but any cooked and shredded beef will do. To counteract the heat of the Red Chilli Sauce, serve soured cream on the side.

INGREDIENTS

375 g/13 oz shredded cooked beef
75 g/3 oz chopped spring onions
675 g/1½ lb Red Chilli Sauce (page 33)
450 g/1 lb grated Cheddar cheese
oil for frying
12 corn tortillas
soured cream

METHOD

▶ Preheat the oven to 180°C/350°F/Gas Mark 4. Have ready a large, shallow baking dish, about 33 x 23 cm/13 x 9 in.

▶ Mix together the beef, spring onions and sauce. Pour the remaining sauce into a wide, shallow dish.

▶ The process here is to fry the tortillas, dip them in red sauce, fill them with the beef mixture and the cheese, roll them, and place them in the baking dish. Set up the utensils and ingredients so you can do this like an assembly line.

▶ Pour oil into a frying pan to a depth of 5 mm/¼ in. Heat until hot, but not smoking, then add the first tortilla. Fry the tortilla just long enough to heat and soften it, 2 to 3 seconds per side. Hold the tortilla just above the pan for a few moments so excess oil can drain off. The heat under the pan should be high enough to reheat the oil after each tortilla, but not so high that it overheats and smokes while you are assembling each enchilada.

▶ Working quickly, dip the tortilla in the sauce so both sides are immersed. Remove the tortilla and let excess sauce drip back into the dish. Lay the tortilla flat. Spread 3 tbsp of the beef mixture in a thin line up the centre of the tortilla, then sprinkle 2 to 3 tbsp grated cheese over the beef. Tightly roll the enchilada into a cylinder and put it, seam-side down, in the baking dish.

▶ Repeat the process with the remaining tortillas and beef, squeezing the enchiladas into a single layer in the baking dish, if possible.

▶ Spoon the remaining sauce over the enchiladas, then sprinkle the remaining cheese over. Bake, uncovered, for 15 minutes. Serve immediately, with soured cream.

Tostadas

Each of these recipes make one tostada

Tostadas began life simply, as crisp, flat tortillas topped with beans, perhaps some meat, shredded lettuce or cabbage, a wedge of tomato, and sometimes cheese and a slice of avocado. Salsa was served on the side. In many restaurants, tostadas have evolved into enormous salads, served in huge bowls of deep-fried flour tortillas. Besides the traditional fillings, they are often made with more exotic ingredients.

At home, tostadas can be a way of using leftovers for a one-person dinner, or they can be the centrepiece of a casual dinner party. The method is the same.

Special equipment is needed to make flour tortillas into bowls, so it is best to keep it simple and stick to corn tortillas that are fried until crisp and laid flat on the plate. If you don't want to parcel out tortillas one by one as they come from the pan, they can be kept in a warm oven for a short time, but really can't be prepared more than 10 or 15 minutes before eating.

INGREDIENTS FOR THE BASE

tortillas
vegetable oil

METHOD

▶ To fry tortillas, heat 5 mm/¼ in of oil in a frying pan. Add a tortilla and cook until crisp, about 1 minute. Drain.

▶ The choice of tostada toppings is unlimited, but here are three combinations to start with. Use your imagination and your own taste to come up with others.

▶ Layer the ingredients on the fried tortilla in the order listed.

INGREDIENTS FOR THE TOPPINGS

TRADITIONAL

50 g/2 oz Chorizo-Bean Dip (page 53) or refried beans
50 g/2 oz shredded cooked beef or chicken
40 g/1½ oz chopped lettuce
40 g/1½ oz grated Cheddar cheese
tomato and avocado wedges
2–3 tbsp Salsa Cruda (pages 18–19)

MODERN

50 g/2 oz torn lettuce
75 g/3 oz Barbecued Chicken (page 110) or Salsa-marinated Flank Steak (page 109), cubed
50 g/2 oz chunks of Cheddar cheese
6 black olives
tomato wedges
2–3 tbsp Avocado Salsa (page 22)

EXOTIC

100 g/4 oz Mango Salsa (page 46) or Nectarine Salsa (page 45)
6 Barbecued Prawns (page 119)

▶ Cut large prawns into bite-sized pieces. Mix with the salsa, then mound onto the tortillas.

Black Bean Chillies Rellenos

Makes 6 first-course servings or
3 main-course servings

Chillies rellenos means stuffed chillies, and in this recipe they are stuffed with spicy black beans and cheese. The rellenos are dipped in beaten egg, then quickly fried – a messy procedure, but worth it. The chillies can be stuffed in advance, then fried at the last minute. Use Anaheims for a mild dish, poblanos for spicier fare, and serve salsa or Red or Green Chilli Sauce (pages 32–3) on the side.

INGREDIENTS

6 large Anaheim or poblano chillies
6 thick slices Cheddar cheese
about 200 g/7 oz Chorizo-Bean Dip
  (page 53)
about 75 g/3 oz cornmeal for dredging
3 eggs, separated
2 tbsp flour
1/4 tsp salt
vegetable oil for frying

METHOD

▶ Barbecue or grill the whole chillies until skin is blistered and partly blackened. Place the chillies in a plastic bag for 10 minutes so their steam can loosen the skins. Remove the skins. Cut a slit along the length of each chilli, and carefully remove the seeds.

▶ Put a slice of cheese in each chilli, then lightly stuff with the bean filling. Dredge the stuffed chilli in cornmeal.

▶ In a medium bowl, beat the egg whites until soft peaks form. In a small bowl, beat the egg yolks with the flour and salt. Fold the yolks into the whites.

▶ Pour oil into a large frying pan to a depth of 1 cm/1/2 in and heat. Dip each chilli into the egg mixture, and use a small rubber spatula to be sure it is thoroughly coated. (*Note:* The fried egg coating will seal the relleno.) Put the relleno in the hot oil and fry until golden, about 1 minute a side. You should fry only 2 rellenos at a time, 3 if you have a very large pan. Do not crowd them.

▶ Drain briefly and serve immediately.

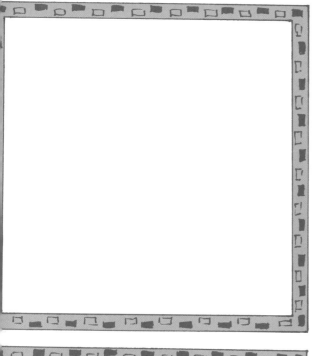

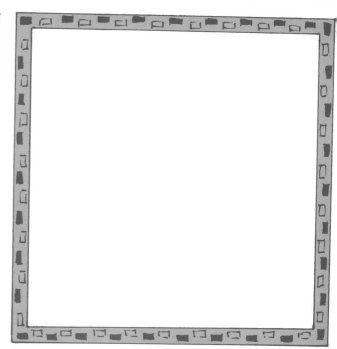

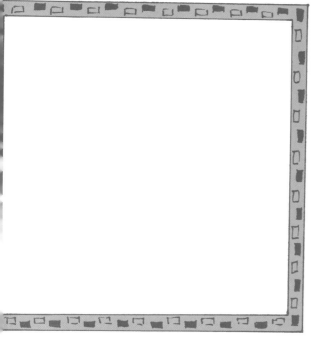

meat dishes

Salsa Chicken
Jerk Chicken
Machaca
Salsa-marinated Flank Steak
Barbecued Chicken
Roast Pork with Chorizo-Rice Stuffing
Chimichurri
Hamburgers
Lamb with Black Bean Salsa

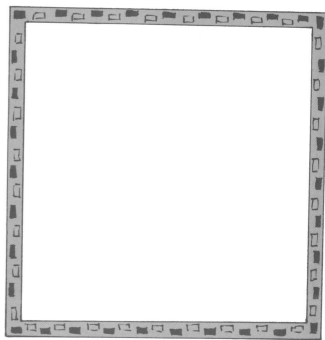

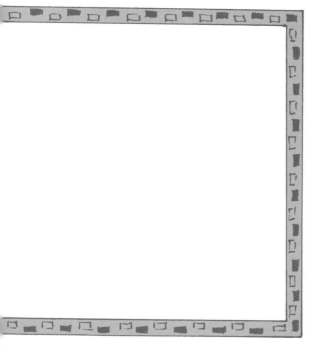

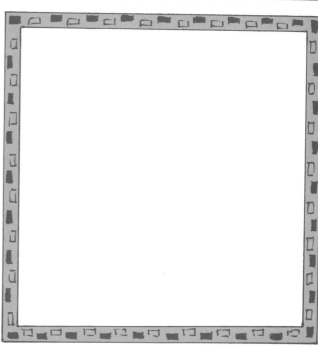

Salsa Chicken

106

Makes 4 servings

Although this recipe calls for boneless chicken breasts, you can use other parts if you adjust the cooking time. You can reduce the cooking time by cutting the chicken into strips or chunks.

INGREDIENTS

25 g/1 oz plain flour
1 tsp ground cumin
1 tsp paprika
½ tsp salt
¼ tsp pepper
4 boneless chicken breast halves
1–2 tbsp vegetable oil
175 g/6 oz tomato-based salsa
about 6 tbsp chicken stock (optional)

METHOD

▶ Mix the flour with the cumin, paprika, salt and pepper. Sprinkle it over the chicken breasts and turn the chicken so all sides are coated with the mixture. Heat the oil in a large frying pan. Add the chicken pieces and brown them on both sides, then stir in the salsa. If the salsa is very thick, add the chicken stock. Simmer the chicken until cooked through, 20 to 30 minutes, occasionally spooning the salsa over the top. Serve over rice or noodles.

Jerk Chicken

Makes 6 servings

Jerk chicken is a Jamaican dish that features the hottest chillies available – the Caribbean Scotch bonnet or its cousin from the Yucatan, the habanero. The chicken is marinated in a paste made of Fiery Habanero Salsa, mustard and herbs, then grilled slowly over indirect heat. The result is very spicy, but if you want truly incendiary chicken, as some jerk chicken is, add another habanero chilli to the paste. In order to cook the chicken long and slow, bone-in pieces such as breasts or thighs are recommended. However, other parts or boneless breasts can also be used if they are carefully watched during cooking. Serve with a fruit salsa, Avocado Salsa (page 22), or a black bean salsa.

Ingredients

75 g/3 oz Fiery Habanero Salsa (page 38)
2 tbsp prepared yellow mustard
1 tbsp dried rosemary or 2 tbsp fresh
1 tbsp dried basil or 3 tbsp fresh
1 tbsp dried thyme or 3 tbsp fresh
2 tbsp fresh lime or orange juice
3 cloves garlic
1 tsp allspice
1 tsp salt
½ tsp pepper
6 chicken breasts or 8–10 chicken thighs

Method

▶ Process all the ingredients except the chicken in a blender or food processor until you have a thick paste. Smear the paste all over the chicken (don't use your bare fingers!), including under the skin if you leave the skin on. Refrigerate for at least 2 hours and up to 12 hours.

▶ Ignite the coals in a barbecue kettle. When the flames have died and the coals are glowing, put the chicken on the greased grid as far from the coals as possible. Cover and let cook. Check the coals every 15 minutes or so, and add new coals if necessary. Turn the chicken once or twice, until the meat is cooked through and the juices run clear when it is pierced with a skewer. This could take as little as 20 minutes for wings or boneless breasts if the fire is hot, or an hour or more for large, unboned pieces and a cooler fire.

107

Machaca

Makes 6 to 8 servings

Machaca is a shredded dried beef dish from northern Mexico. Traditional recipes call for the beef to be air-dried for several days before it is cooked and shredded, but in this recipe, it is simply simmered long and slow, then shredded and baked. Most of the work can be done a day in advance. Serve Machaca with warm flour tortillas and Black Bean-Sweetcorn Salsa (page 36) or any salsa of your choice. Leftovers are marvellous in Quesadillas (page 96) or scrambled eggs.

108

INGREDIENTS

1.5 kg/3 lb chuck steak, brisket of beef or other cut
1 tbsp ground cumin
2 tsp dried oregano
1 tsp salt
1 tsp pepper
1–2 tbsp vegetable oil
1 onion, peeled and cut into wedges
450 g/1 lb Salsa Cruda (pages 18–19) or Chipotle Salsa (page 34)
2 eggs, lightly beaten with a fork

METHOD

► Trim any excess fat from the beef. Mix together the cumin, oregano, salt and pepper, and rub this mixture over the surface of the roast. Let stand for 30 minutes to allow the flavours to develop.

► Heat the oil in a deep frying pan or Dutch oven. Add the meat and brown it on all sides. Add the onion and water to a depth of 1 inch. Bring the water to the boil, then cover the pan and reduce the heat to a simmer. Or you can transfer the pan to the oven and cook at 180°C/350°F/Gas Mark 4. Allow the meat to cook until it is tender and falling from the bone, about 2½ hours. Check occasionally during cooking and add more water if needed.

► When the meat is done, cut it into several large pieces and let it cool slightly. When it is cool enough to handle, use 2 forks to pull the meat apart into shreds. It is easier to shred the meat while it is still very warm.

► Spread the shredded meat on a large baking sheet and bake in a preheated 180°C/350°F/ Gas Mark 4 oven, 12 to 15 minutes, turning once or twice, until it is dry. The meat may be prepared in advance to this point, then refrigerated until just before serving time.

► Put the meat in a large frying pan with the salsa and cook over medium heat. Let it simmer for about 10 minutes so that any excess moisture in the salsa evaporates. Add the beaten eggs and cook, stirring well, so there are strands of egg mixed through the meat. Serve immediately with warm flour tortillas and salsa.

Salsa-marinated Flank Steak

Makes 4 to 6 servings

A salsa marinade adds flavour to flank steak, or any other thick cut of beef that you like to barbecue. Cook the beef, then slice it thinly. Serve with salad, warm tortillas, and a choice of salsas – perhaps Avocado Salsa (page 22) and Grilled Salsa (page 26).

INGREDIENTS

50 g/2 oz cooked or puréed tomato-based salsa, such as Basic Cooked Salsa (page 32) or Barbecued Salsa (page 26)
4 tbsp dry red wine
4 tbsp vegetable oil
3 cloves garlic, minced
900 g/2 ob flank steak or other cut of beef

METHOD

▶ Combine all the ingredients except the beef and mix well. Put the beef in a sturdy plastic food-storage bag. Add the marinade to the bag and make sure the beef is fully coated. Tie the end of the bag, then refrigerate for at least 4 hours and up to 24 hours, turning occasionally.

▶ About 90 minutes before you want to eat, start a fire in the barbecue kettle. When the flames have died and the coals are glowing, remove the meat from the bag and place it on an oiled grid directly over the coals. Cooking over the coals will char the outside of the steak while the inside cooks slowly. However,

if drips cause too many flare-ups, you may wish to move the meat off to the side and cover the kettle.

▶ Cooking time will depend on the thickness of the meat, the distance above the coals, and the heat of the coals. For meat that is 4 cm/ 1½ in thick, cook for at least 7 minutes a side, then check if cooked to required degree. It may take as long as 15 minutes a side.

▶ When the meat is done, remove it from the grid and let it stand for 10 to 20 minutes for ease of carving. Cutting against the grain, slice the meat thinly and serve.

109

Barbecued Chicken

Makes 4 servings

In this recipe, chicken breasts are marinated in a simple, spicy, citrus marinade, then barbecued over hot coals. It is a dish that tastes excellent hot or cold. It's also delicious cut into chunks and served on a green salad, topped with salsa – Avocado Salsa (page 22) and Nectarine Salsa (page 45) are particularly good.

INGREDIENTS

6 tbsp olive oil
2 tbsp fresh lime juice
3 tbsp fresh orange juice
2 cloves garlic, minced
1 tbsp chopped fresh coriander
¼ tsp hot pepper sauce
4 boneless chicken breast halves, with or
*   without skin*
1 tsp freshly ground black pepper
175 g/6 oz salsa of your choice

METHOD

▶ Make a marinade by mixing together all the ingredients except the chicken, the salsa and the black pepper. Put the chicken in a plastic or glass bowl and pour the marinade over it. Turn the chicken breasts so they are thoroughly coated, then let marinate, refrigerated, for at least 6 hours or overnight. Turn the chicken 2 or 3 times while it is marinating. Just before cooking, sprinkle with the black pepper.

▶ About an hour before serving time, start the fire in the barbecue. When the flames have died, and the coals are glowing and covered with white ash (about 40 minutes), put the chicken breasts on the greased grid over the coals. Barbecue, turning once, until the chicken is cooked through, about 12 minutes, depending on the thickness of the meat and the distance from the coals. Serve with salsa on top or on the side.

110

New Mexico chillies in their red and green stages.

Roast Pork with Chorizo-Rice Stuffing

Makes 6 servings

Pork loin is stuffed with a spicy chorizo-rice stuffing, then spread with salsa and roasted. Use any vegetable salsa of your choice. Fiery Habanero Salsa (page 38) infuses the meat with the heat of the chillies, while milder salsas let the other flavours show through. Roast Jalapeño Salsa (page 16) is a good, though messy choice. Chunkier salsas, such as Salsa Cruda III (page 19), have a tendency to fall off.

INGREDIENTS

1/4 tsp salt
2 tsp olive oil or butter
200 g/7 oz white rice
175–225 g/6–8 oz chorizo sausage
75 g/3 oz chopped onion
2 cloves garlic, minced
40 g/1 1/2 oz toasted pine nuts (see below)
1 kg/2 1/4 lb pork loin
300 g/11 oz salsa

METHOD

▶ Preheat the oven to 180°C/350°F/Gas Mark 4. Put 475 ml/16 fl oz water in a saucepan, add the salt and olive oil or butter and bring to the boil. Stir in the rice, cover and reduce the heat. Cook until the water has been absorbed and the rice is tender, 15 to 20 minutes.

▶ Meanwhile, crumble the chorizo into a small frying pan. Cook over medium heat until the sausage is browned, 7 to 10 minutes, then remove with a slotted spoon and set aside. Discard all but 1 tbsp of fat. Reheat the fat and add the onion. Sauté for 5 minutes, then add the garlic and pine nuts, and cook for 1 minute. Remove from the heat. Mix the chorizo and the onion mixture into the cooked rice.

▶ Unroll the pork loin, or make several lengthwise cuts so that it opens as much as possible into a thick, flat piece. Spoon some

rice mixture into the centre of the loin, then reroll the meat and tie with string. You will have some rice left over. Put it in a lightly greased baking dish, cover and set aside.

▶ Put the pork, cut side up, on a rack in a small roasting tin. Spread some of the salsa over the pork, coating it as much as possible, but make sure you have some salsa left over for basting. Put the pork in the oven and cook for approximately 1 hour, until the internal temperature measured with a meat thermometer reaches 71°C/160°F (although the meat is safe at 60°C/140°). Baste the meat

at least once with the additional salsa. During the last 5 minutes of cooking, put the leftover rice stuffing in the oven.

▶ When the pork is done, remove it from the oven and let stand for 15 minutes before carving it into slices. Let the stuffing continue to cook while the pork rests.

To toast pine nuts: Spread them in a single layer on a baking sheet. Bake at 180°C/350°F/Gas Mark 4 for 5 to 10 minutes until they are golden brown. Watch pine nuts carefully as they burn very quickly.

Chimichurri

113

Makes 6 servings

Chimichurri is Argentinian barbecued beef
served with a parsley-vinegar salsa. Beef steaks
(usually fillet or rib steaks) are marinated in a
simple mixture, such as a saltwater brine, salt and
lemon juice, or just salt and pepper. Sometimes
they are marinated in Chimichurri Salsa. This
salsa varies widely. Typically it is thinner than
most salsas, and includes vinegar, olive oil, garlic,
onion and parsley. However, lime juice or orange
juice – especially bitter orange – is frequently
substituted for all or part of the vinegar. A small
amount of oregano may take the place of parsley,
and fresh or ground dried chillies are optional.

If you wish to marinate the beef in
Chimichurri Salsa before cooking, make a double
portion of salsa. Discard any excess marinade and
serve the cooked beef with fresh Chimichurri
Salsa. Marinade that has been in contact with raw
beef should not be eaten unless it is boiled first.

INGREDIENTS

6 beef steaks
salt and pepper
3 cloves garlic, minced
Chimichurri Salsa (recipe follows)

METHOD

▶ Sprinkle the beef with salt and pepper, then
rub with the minced garlic. Allow to stand for
an hour or longer in the refrigerator.
Meanwhile, prepare the barbecue. When the
barbecue coals are glowing and the flames
have barely died, cook the meat until it is done
to your liking. Serve with Chimichurri Salsa.

INGREDIENTS FOR CHIMICHURRI SALSA

175 ml/6 fl oz good-quality olive oil
3 tbsp red wine vinegar
40 g/1½ oz chopped fresh parsley
1 tsp dried oregano
1 jalapeño chilli, chopped
5 cloves garlic, minced
2 tbsp minced onion
½ tsp salt
¼ tsp pepper

METHOD

▶ Combine all the ingredients. You may chop
them briefly in a food processor, if desired. Let
stand for at least 30 minutes before serving.

Hamburgers

Makes 1 serving

Is there an ingredient that hasn't been tried on hamburgers? Salsa is a popular addition, either as a condiment or mixed in with the meat. Here are some ideas for combining salsa and hamburgers.

METHOD

► Mix 1 to 2 tbsp salsa with 150 g/5 oz ground beef before making into patties. Any tomato-based or tomatillo salsa is good, but Tomato-Mint Salsa (page 24) adds an unexpected twist. Roast Jalapeño Salsa (page 16) is also a good addition.

► Spoon salsa over the cooked meat or spread it on the bun. In addition to the above salsas, Sweet Red Pepper (page 20) and Olive Salsa (page 22) go well with hamburgers.

► Make an avocado burger by topping the cooked meat with Guacamole (page 17) or Avocado Salsa (page 22).

► For an unusual sandwich, serve the burger open-faced with Black Bean Salsa (page 26). Or for a tropical touch, try Pineapple-Ginger Salsa (page 42).

Lamb with Black Bean Salsa

Makes 6 servings

In this Brazilian-inspired dish, a leg of lamb is marinated, then roasted or barbecued, and served with salsa. It is a fairly easy dish that requires a minimum of last-minute work.

INGREDIENTS

leg of lamb, about 2.25 kg/5 lb (see Note below)
4 tbsp olive oil
3 tbsp red wine vinegar
2 tbsp fresh orange juice
4 cloves garlic, minced
1 tsp dried oregano
½ tsp dried rosemary
50 g/2 oz finely chopped onion
250 g/9 oz Black Bean Salsa (page 26) or Black Bean-Papaya Salsa (page 46)

METHOD

► Put the lamb in a non-metallic dish. To make a marinade, combine all the remaining ingredients except the salsa. Pour the marinade over the lamb, making sure that the entire surface is coated. Marinate the lamb in the refrigerator for at least 2 hours and up to 24 hours, turning it occasionally and spooning marinade over it.

► Roast the lamb in a 180°C/350°F/Gas Mark 4 oven or over a grill. Lamb is cooked rare when it reaches an internal temperature of 60°C/140°F (test with a meat thermometer) – about 20 minutes per pound in the oven, considerably less time on a grill. Lamb is traditionally served rare or medium rare

(about 66°C/150°F). It is easier to carve if it is allowed to rest for about 20 minutes after it comes out of the oven. Serve with the salsa.

Note: Weight is for unboned meat. If you plan to barbecue the lamb, ask the butcher to remove the bone and butterfly the meat so it lies relatively flat.

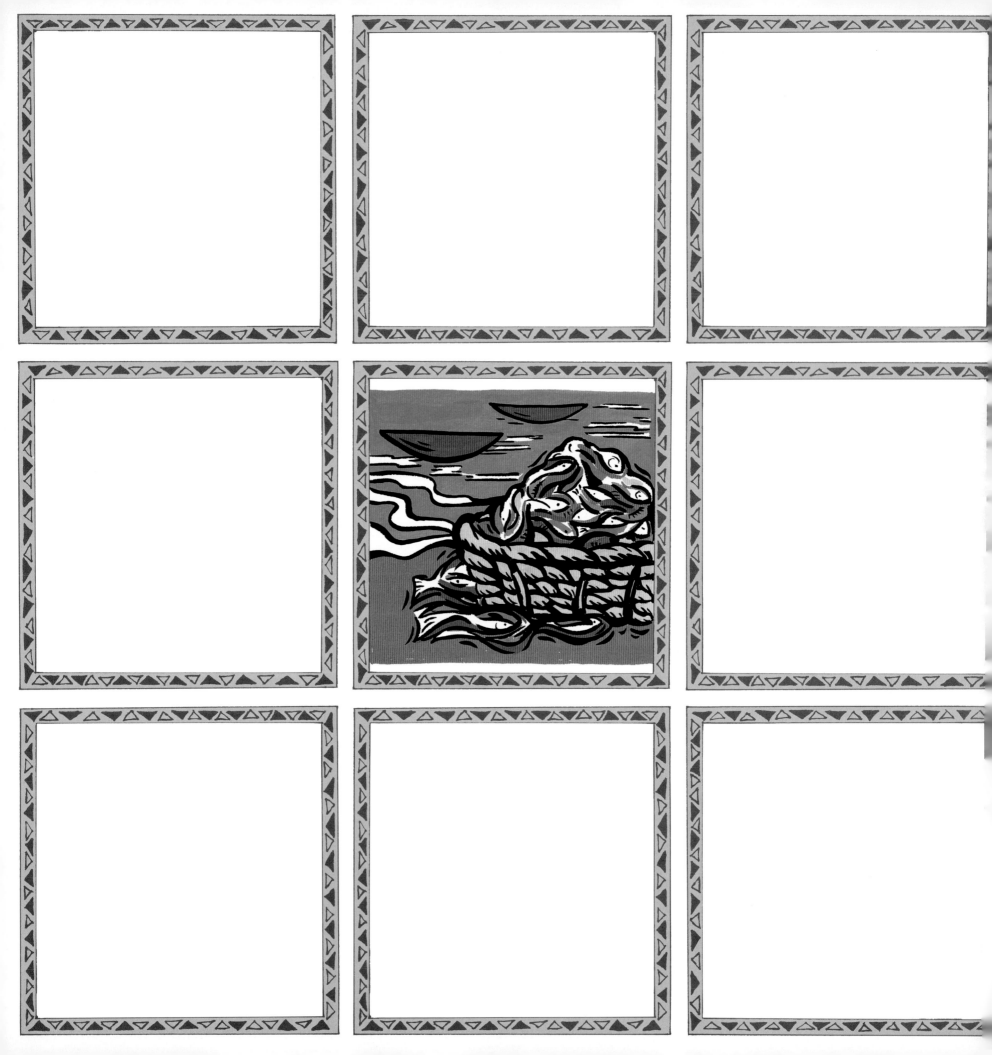

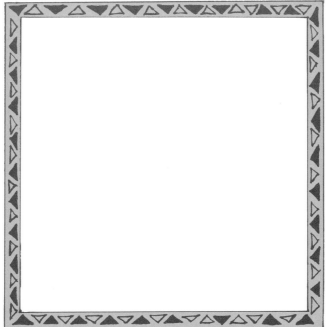
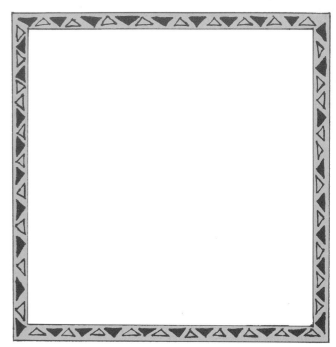

seafood dishes

Ceviche
Barbecued Prawns
Red Snapper Veracruz
Barbecued Clams
Prawns in Chipotle Salsa
Barbecued Salmon
Prawn-stuffed Green Peppers

Ceviche

Makes 2 to 3 servings

In this speciality dish from Central and South America, raw fish or shellfish is marinated in spices and lemon or lime juice until the citrus "cooks" the seafood. This version uses a habanero chilli for extra heat. (If you can't find a habanero, substitute 2 serrano chillies.) Ceviche can be served like prawn cocktail, or spooned over lettuce for a salad. Be sure to use extremely fresh, high-quality seafood.

INGREDIENTS

*225 g/8 oz white fish fillets, prawns or
    scallops, or a combination*
175 ml/6 fl oz fresh lime juice
175 g/6 oz Salsa Cruda III (page 19)
½ sweet red pepper, cut into strips
*1 habanero chilli, cut crosswise into thin
    rings*
1 tbsp white vinegar
2 tbsp olive oil

METHOD

► Clean the seafood as needed; peel and devein prawns, if using. Cut into bite-sized pieces. If you are using large prawns, cut them into 2 or 3 pieces so the lime juice can penetrate evenly. Mix the remaining ingredients in a non-metallic bowl, then stir in the seafood pieces so all are evenly coated. Refrigerate for at least 6 hours, until the seafood turns opaque, as if cooked.

118

Barbecued Prawns

Makes 4 main-course servings or
6 first-course servings

Marinated and barbecued prawns served with salsa make a delicious appetizer or light main course. For variety, serve them with Barbecued Clams (page 120) and two or three salsas. Try any traditional tomato-based salsa, one of the sweetcorn salsas, or Nectarine Salsa (page 45).

INGREDIENTS

*450 g/1 lb medium to large prawns, shelled
    and deveined*
6 tbsp olive oil
3 cloves garlic, minced
3 tbsp fresh lime juice
2 tbsp chopped fresh basil or 2 tsp dried
1 tsp red pepper flakes

METHOD

▶ Place the prawns in a glass or plastic bowl. Mix together all the remaining ingredients. Pour this marinade over the prawns and stir, making sure that all the prawns are thoroughly coated. Marinate, refrigerated, for 2 to 4 hours, stirring 2 or 3 times.

▶ About 45 minutes before you want to eat, start the barbecue fire. If you plan to use wooden skewers, soak them in water for at least 30 minutes so they don't burn easily. A few minutes before the coals are ready, thread the prawns loosely on the skewers. If they are crammed together, they will not cook evenly.

▶ When the flames have died down and the coals are glowing and covered with white ash, place the prawns on the greased grid. They will cook quickly, especially if dripping marinade causes flare-ups, so they need to be closely watched. Barbecue, turning once, until cooked through, about 2 to 4 minutes a side, depending on the size of the prawns and the distance from the coals. The prawns will lose their translucency and turn an opaque white-pink. Do not overcook them, or they will get tough. Serve with salsas of your choice.

Red Snapper Veracruz

Makes 4 servings

In this version of a traditional Mexican recipe the fish is fried briefly, then simmered in a tomato salsa. It is good served over plain rice or on its own.

INGREDIENTS

4 fillets of red snapper, about 175 g/6 oz each
salt and pepper
4 tbsp flour
2 tbsp vegetable oil
350 g/12 oz Salsa Cruda I (page 18) or Salsa
  Cruda III (page 19)

½ sweet red pepper, cut into strips
1 or 2 jalapeño chillies, seeded and cut into
  rings
chopped spring onions
1 tbsp chopped fresh coriander

METHOD

► Season the fish fillets with salt and pepper, then dust with the flour. Heat the oil in a frying pan, add the fillets and cook them quickly, so that each side is lightly browned.

► Add the salsa, red pepper and jalapeños to the pan. Simmer over low heat, spooning the salsa over the fish. Cook until the fish flakes easily, about 10 minutes per 2.5 cm/1 in of thickness.

► Put the fish onto serving plates, spooning salsa, red pepper strips and jalapeño rings over each piece. Garnish with the spring onions and coriander.

120

Barbecued Clams

Few dishes beat Barbecued Clams for simplicity. Serve them as an appetizer, cooking them on the grill before the main course goes on the fire, or as a main course by themselves or with Barbecued Prawns (page 119). They are good with Salsa Cruda I (page 18), Nectarine Salsa (page 45), or Corn Salsa (page 21) on the side.

INGREDIENTS

4 to 6 clams per person for an appetizer;
  12 per person for a main course
salsa of your choice
melted butter and garlic (optional)

METHOD

► Scrub the clam shells clean under cool running water. Discard any clams that are not tightly closed or don't close tightly under the running water. When the barbecue coals are glowing and the flames have died, place the clams on the grid over the coals. A screen for cooking small items is handy, to ensure the clams don't slip through the grid. Cook until the clam shells pop open, 5 to 10 minutes.

► In addition to salsa, serve a bowl of butter melted with a little garlic for dipping.

Prawns in Chipotle Salsa

Makes 4 servings

Lime-marinated prawns are sautéed, then cooked briefly in Chipotle Salsa, which imparts its hot, smoky flavour to the prawns. Serve them on their own or over plain white rice. If you don't have time to make Chipotle Salsa, make Winter Salsa II (page 39), which uses canned chipotle chillies, while the prawns are marinating.

Ingredients

6 tbsp olive oil
4 tbsp fresh lime juice
3 cloves garlic, minced
575 g/1¼ lb medium or large prawns, peeled and deveined
250 g/9 oz Chipotle Salsa (page 34)
½ tsp salt

Method

▶ Mix together 2 tbsp olive oil, the lime juice and garlic to make a marinade. Put the prawns in a glass or other non-reactive bowl. Pour the marinade over the prawns, and toss so that all the pieces are coated. Let marinate for 30 minutes.

▶ Heat the remaining oil in a large frying pan. Remove the prawns from the bowl, reserving the marinade. Add the prawns to the oil and sauté quickly over medium heat for about 1½ minutes. Remove the prawns and set aside. Add the Chipotle Salsa to the remaining oil and fry it, stirring almost constantly, for 5 minutes. Add the marinade and salt, and cook for another 2 minutes. Return the prawns to the skillet and cook for about 2 minutes longer, just long enough to cook through the prawns and let them absorb some of the salsa flavours.

121

Barbecued Salmon

Makes 4 servings

Salmon is marinated in a chilli vinaigrette, then barbecued or grilled. It is delicious served with Black Bean-Sweetcorn Salsa (page 36), or with a fruit salsa. This recipe also works well with the more substantial white fish like halibut and swordfish.

INGREDIENTS

1 poblano chilli
6 tbsp olive oil
2 tbsp red wine vinegar
2 cloves garlic, peeled
1 tbsp chopped fresh coriander
1½ lb salmon fillet
salsa of your choice

METHOD

▶ Cut the poblano chilli in quarters lengthwise, remove the stem, seeds and veins. Grill the chilli, skin side up, until skin is blackened. Put the chilli in a small plastic bag or pouch of aluminium foil for 10 minutes, then peel off the skin. It's all right if a few bits of blackened skin remain. Put the chilli in a blender or food processor with all the remaining ingredients except the salmon and salsa. Purée.

▶ Put the salmon in a shallow glass or other non-reactive dish and pour the purée over it. Turn the salmon to make sure it is completely coated, then marinate in the refrigerator for 1 to 4 hours.

▶ Preheat the grill, or start a fire in the barbecue and wait until the flames have died and the coals are glowing. Place the salmon on a lightly oiled grill pan and put under the grill, or place on an oiled grid over the coals. Cook, turning once, until barely cooked through, about 8 minutes total, depending on the thickness of the fish. Serve with salsa on top or on the side.

Prawn-stuffed Green Peppers

Makes 4 servings

These sweet peppers are stuffed with a tasty mixture of rice, prawns, salsa and soured cream, then baked. They make an excellent lunch or light supper dish. For extra flavour, cook the prawns in Chipotle Salsa (page 34).

INGREDIENTS

4 green sweet peppers
675 g/1¹/₂ lb cooked white rice
225 g/8 oz cooked prawns, cleaned and cut
  into bite-sized pieces
175 g/6 oz Salsa Cruda (see pages 18–19)
250 ml/8 fl oz soured cream
chopped spring onion
¹/₂ tsp ground cumin
1 tsp salt (optional)

METHOD

▶ Preheat the oven to 180°C/350°F/Gas Mark 4. Lightly oil a shallow baking dish, about 23 x 23 cm/9 x 9 inches.

▶ Cut the tops off the peppers and reserve. Wash the peppers and clean out the seeds and membranes. Bring a large saucepan of water to the boil, and add the peppers. Boil for 2 minutes, then remove and drain.

▶ Combine all the remaining ingredients, adding the salt, if the rice was cooked without salt. Stuff this mixture into the peppers, then stand them in the baking dish. Put the tops back on the peppers and bake for about 40 minutes, until tender.

vegetarian dishes

Polenta with Black Bean Salsa
Huevos Rancheros
Deluxe Huevos Rancheros
Cheese Salsa Omelette
South-western Frittata
Cornmeal Pancakes
with Black Beans
Double-Salsa with
Black-eyed Beans

Polenta with Black Bean Salsa

Makes about 6 servings

This is a hybrid dish, combining Italian polenta with South-western Black Bean Salsa. Serve it for lunch or a light dinner. The polenta must be prepared in advance. Traditional polenta – a coarse grind of cornmeal – needs cooking for at least 30 minutes, but now quick-cooking polentas are available; however, they taste better if you cook them for 10 minutes longer than recommended on the packet.

INGREDIENTS

Polenta (recipe follows)
olive oil for frying or grilling
350 g/12 oz Cheddar cheese, thinly sliced
250 g/9 oz Black Bean Salsa (page 26)

METHOD

► Cut the polenta into slices about 4 cm/ 1½ in thick. If you are going to barbecue it, lightly brush the cut edges with olive oil. If you are going to fry it, heat 1 tbsp olive oil in a frying pan.

► When the oil is hot, or when the barbecue coals are glowing and the flames have died, put the polenta slices on the heat. Cook until the bottom is golden (if frying) or charred with grid marks, about 3 minutes. Turn the polenta and put the sliced cheese on top. Cook until the underneath is golden or charred. (*Note:* If you are frying the polenta, the cheese will melt more readily if you use a lid on the skillet. Add more oil if necessary before frying next batch of polenta.)

► Remove the polenta from the heat. Spoon the Black Bean Salsa over the top, and serve.

INGREDIENTS FOR POLENTA

2 tsp salt
275 g/10 oz polenta

METHOD

► Lightly oil a loaf tin, about 9 x 5 inches. Bring 1.25 litres/2¼ pints water and the salt to the boil in a large saucepan. Slowly add the polenta, stirring constantly and watching for lumps. Cook over low heat, stirring almost constantly, 30 minutes or so, until the polenta forms a thick mass that pulls cleanly away from the sides of pan. Pour the polenta into the loaf tin and smooth the top. Let it cool for at least 30 minutes before turning out.

126

Huevos Rancheros

Makes 4 servings

Huevos Rancheros is a traditional Mexican breakfast dish, with as many variations as there are families. This is a simple version made with tortillas, fried eggs, cheese and salsa. Any tomato or tomatillo salsa is suitable, or try a black bean salsa for a change. For a heartier breakfast, fry 2 eggs per serving. Since this dish is made in steps, use heatproof plates, and keep them warm in the oven between steps.

INGREDIENTS

200 g/7 oz salsa of your choice
oil for frying

4 corn tortillas
4 eggs
100 g/4 oz grated Cheddar cheese
chopped spring onions and coriander for
garnish

METHOD

▶ Heat the oven to 110°C/225°F/Gas Mark ¼ and put the plates in to warm. Warm the salsa in a small saucepan over low heat.

▶ Heat a little oil in a frying pan. Fry the tortillas, one at a time, for a few seconds per side, just enough to soften. Drain each tortilla and put on a plate in the oven.

▶ Discard all but 1 tbsp oil. Keep the heat at medium. Break the eggs onto saucers, and slide them into the hot oil. Cook for 2 or 3 minutes until the yolks are set, spooning hot oil over the top of the eggs or covering the pan to keep the heat in. If desired, turn the eggs and cook for about 30 seconds longer.

▶ Put 1 egg on each tortilla. Top with salsa and sprinkle the cheese over the top. Garnish with spring onions and coriander.

Deluxe Huevos Rancheros

Makes 4 servings

This is a heartier version than the previous one, beginning with a simple quesadilla that is topped with beans. The eggs are poached in salsa. This version needs a fairly liquid tomato salsa, such as any Salsa Cruda (pages 18–19), or Basic Cooked Salsa (page 32). For extra flavour, try Chipotle Salsa (page 34) or Winter Salsa II (page 39), which is made with chipotle chillies.

INGREDIENTS

8 flour tortillas
225 g/8 oz grated Cheddar cheese
vegetable oil or melted butter
350 g/12 oz refried beans
450 g/1 lb salsa of your choice
8 eggs
chopped tomatoes and black olives for
garnish

METHOD

▶ Preheat the oven to 180°C/350°F/Gas Mark 4. Lightly oil 2 baking sheets.

▶ Place 4 tortillas on the baking sheets and sprinkle each one with 25 g/1 oz cheese, evenly spread over the entire tortilla. Place a second tortilla on top of the cheese and press down. Lightly brush the top of the second tortilla with oil or melted butter. Bake for 5 to 8 minutes until the cheese is barely melted. Reduce the oven heat to warm.

▶ Fry the beans in a scant amount of oil, just to heat through. Spread some beans on top of each quesadilla. Return the quesadillas to the oven to keep warm.

▶ Put half the salsa in a medium frying pan and heat for 2 to 3 minutes. Break 4 eggs onto saucers and slide them into the salsa. Cover and poach for about 3 minutes. Put 2 eggs each on 2 quesadillas and divide the sauce between them. Repeat with the remaining 4 eggs and salsa. Or you may poach all the eggs at the same time in 2 pans.

▶ Sprinkle the remaining cheese over the eggs. Garnish with some chopped tomatoes and olives.

128

Mexican children enjoying tortillas.

Cheese Salsa Omelette

Makes 1 serving

Eggs and salsa are a great combination, and here are two omelettes that incorporate the salsa right into the cooking. Use your imagination to create other variations.

INGREDIENTS

2 or 3 eggs
pinch of salt
few drops of hot pepper sauce
butter or oil for frying
25 g/1 oz grated Cheddar cheese
2 tbsp tomato-based salsa, plus extra to serve
2 slices of avocado

METHOD

▶ Beat the eggs, salt and hot pepper sauce together with a fork just until blended. Heat about 1 to 2 teaspoons butter or oil in an 18–20cm/7–8-in frying pan, pour in the eggs and shake the pan a little so they spread evenly across the bottom. As the egg curls around the edges, lift the edge slightly with a fork or knife and tilt the pan so that the uncooked egg runs from the centre and under the cooked egg. Continue lifting and tilting until all the liquid egg has run over the edges and set, but the centre is still soft. Sprinkle the cheese in a 5-cm/2-in wide band up the centre, then spoon the salsa over the cheese. Use a spatula to fold one-third of the omelette over the cheese. Now, as you ease the omelette out of the pan and onto a serving plate, fold the other third over the centre. Garnish with the avocado and serve with extra salsa on the side.

Variation: Instead of salsa, spread 3 tbsp warmed Hot Bean Dip (page 52) up the centre of the omelette. Sprinkle cheese over the beans, then top with 2 tbsp soured cream.

South-western Frittata

Makes 4 to 6 servings

A frittata is a one-dish meal of eggs, cheese, and fried potatoes, seasoned with salsa. It is similar to an omelette, but is baked in the oven and is large enough to serve several people. This recipe is particularly good with any of the salsas in which barbecued or roast chillies or sweet peppers are the primary ingredient, such as Roast Jalapeño Salsa (page 16) or Sweet Red Pepper Salsa (page 20). For this dish, you will need an ovenproof frying pan of about 1.25-litre/2¾-pint capacity. If you don't have such a pan, fry the potatoes, onions and salsa, then transfer them to a casserole and add the remaining ingredients.

INGREDIENTS

vegetable oil for frying
300 g/11 oz peeled and diced potato
175 g/6 oz chopped onion
175 g/6 oz salsa of your choice, plus extra for
* serving*
100 g/4 oz grated Cheddar cheese
6 eggs
2 tbsp milk
1 tsp salt
¼ tsp pepper

METHOD

► Heat the oil in a frying pan. Add the potato and onion and fry until golden, about 15 minutes. (Or you can boil the potatoes until they are barely tender, then dice and fry.) Add the salsa. If you are using a tomato-based salsa, let it simmer for 5 minutes or so to cook off any excess liquid. Remove from the heat. Preheat the oven to 200°C/400°F/Gas Mark 6.

► Sprinkle the grated cheese over the potatoes and onions. Break the eggs into a bowl, add the milk, salt and pepper and beat lightly. Pour this mixture over the potatoes. Bake the frittata in the pan until the eggs have puffed up, the centre is set and the edges are golden, about 15 minutes. Cut into wedges and serve with additional salsa on the side.

Cornmeal Pancakes with Black Beans

132

Makes 15 to 18 10-cm/4-in pancakes, or 6 to 8 servings

This savoury dish, excellent for brunch, features thin, crisp-edged cornmeal pancakes topped with spicy black beans, salsa and soured cream. The beans, salsa and pancake batter can be made the night before.

INGREDIENTS

Cornmeal Pancakes (recipe follows)
400 g/14 oz Hot Bean Dip (made with
  vegetarian refried beans)
175 g/6 oz Salsa Cruda of choice
  (pages 18–19)
350 ml/12 fl oz soured cream

METHOD

► Make the pancakes as directed below. Heat the bean dip. When the pancakes are cooked, spoon some bean dip on each, add a little salsa, and top with a dollop of soured cream.

INGREDIENTS FOR CORNMEAL PANCAKES

50 g/2 oz plain flour
100 g/4 oz cornmeal
1 tsp baking powder
1 tsp bicarbonate of soda
1 tsp salt
350 ml/12 fl oz buttermilk
3 tbsp melted butter
2 eggs, lightly beaten with fork
oil for frying

METHOD

► Combine the dry ingredients in a medium bowl. Mix together the buttermilk, melted butter and eggs, then stir into the dry ingredients. Mix by hand until the ingredients are combined but the batter is still slightly lumpy.

► Heat a scant amount of oil in a frying pan, barely enough to coat the pan lightly. Spoon in small amounts of batter, tilting the pan so the batter spreads out to make thin pancakes. Cook over medium heat until the underside is golden brown, then turn and cook the other side. Don't crowd the pancakes. Use 2 pans at once if you wish. Add oil as needed, but only in tiny amounts.

Double-Salsa with Black-eyed Beans

Makes 6 to 8 servings

This is a vegetarian version of Hopping John, the black-eyed bean and rice dish that Southerners eat for good luck on New Year's Day. Instead of simmering the beans with ham, mix the cooked beans with Chipotle Salsa, which gives them a hot, smoky flavour that substitutes well for meat. The rice and bean mixture is topped with a chunky raw salsa that adds colour, a crunchy texture, and the flavour of tomatoes and onions.

Ingredients

350 g/12 oz dried black-eyed beans
300 g/11 oz Chipotle Salsa (page 34)
1–2 tsp salt
$^1\!/_2$ tsp pepper
1.5 kg/3 lb cooked white rice
about 350 g/12 oz Salsa Cruda III (page 19)
40 g/1$^1\!/_2$ oz chopped spring onions

Method

▶ Sort through the beans for pebbles or other debris, then put the beans in a large saucepan with 1.75 litres/3 pints water. Bring to the boil, cover and boil for 2 minutes, then turn off the heat and let the beans stand for an hour.

▶ Drain and rinse the beans. Rinse the saucepan, then put the beans back in the pan and add enough water to cover them by 7.5 cm/3 in. Bring to the boil, then cook over low heat until most of the water has evaporated and the beans are tender. Add the Chipotle Salsa, salt, and pepper during the last few minutes of cooking.

▶ Put the rice in bowls and spoon the beans over the rice. Stir the spring onions into the Salsa Cruda, then top the beans with this mixture.

desserts

Honey-Ginger Peach Salsa
Tropical Dessert Salsa
Fruit Salsa Romanoff
Banana Salsa
Salsa Ice Cream
Sopapillas
Cookie Cups with Ricotta Cream
and Fruit Salsa

Honey-Ginger Peach Salsa

Makes about 575 g/1¼ lb

This dessert salsa is good spooned over ice cream, used as a filling in Sopapillas (page 141), or in Cookie Cups with Ricotta Cream (page 142). Or use it as the flavouring in homemade ice cream (page 140). You can substitute nectarines for the peaches if you wish.

INGREDIENTS

500 g/18 oz ripe peaches, peeled, stoned and cut into 5-mm/¼-in dice
1 jalapeño chilli, unseeded, minced
1 tsp minced fresh ginger
1 tbsp honey
2 tbsp fresh orange juice
½ tsp cinnamon

METHOD

▶ Combine all the ingredients. Let stand for at least 30 minutes to allow the flavours to develop.

Tropical Dessert Salsa

Makes about 575 g/1¼ lb

This is a sweet salsa, with a touch of spiciness from the chilli powder. Adjust the amount of chilli powder depending on how hot you want the salsa and whether you are using commercial chilli powder or ground dried chillies. For variety, add a tablespoon of chopped fresh mint. Like the other dessert salsas, it is good over or in ice cream (page 140), on Sopapillas (page 141) or in Cookie Cups with Ricotta Cream (page 142).

Ingredients

1 mango, peeled, stoned and cut into 5-mm/ ¼-in dice
150 g/5 oz cantaloupe, cut into 5-mm/¼-in dice
150 g/5 oz fresh pineapple, cut into 5-mm/ ¼-in dice
1 tbsp brown sugar
about 1 tsp chilli powder, to taste
1 tbsp each fresh orange and lime juice

Method

▶ Combine all the ingredients. Let stand for 30 minutes, then taste and adjust the seasonings.

Fruit Salsa Romanoff

138

Makes about 350 g/12 oz

This dessert salsa takes advantage of whatever seasonal fruits are available, but it traditionally includes at least some strawberries. Spoon it over ice cream or pound cake.

INGREDIENTS

50–75 g/2–3 oz sugar
4 tbsp fresh orange juice
2 tbsp orange liqueur or cognac (optional)
350 g/12 oz sliced or diced fruit, including at least 75 g/3 oz strawberries, and your choice of peaches, plums, nectarines, apricots, cherries, seedless grapes, raspberries, or other fruit

METHOD

► Mix together the sugar, orange juice and liqueur, adjusting the amount of sugar according to the sweetness of the fruit. Put the fruit in a bowl, pour the marinade over it and stir gently. Chill for at least 1 hour, stirring occasionally.

Banana Salsa

Makes enough salsa for 4 to 6 servings of ice cream

Perhaps this recipe is cheating a little! It's called Banana Salsa because the bananas are chopped and cooked with seasonings, but it's really a sort of chopped Bananas Foster, served over ice cream. Nevertheless, when the result is this delicious, who's going to quibble over a name?

INGREDIENTS

vanilla ice cream
3 tbsp butter
3 tbsp brown sugar
$\frac{1}{2}$ tsp cinnamon
3 tbsp rum, orange liqueur or orange juice
2 medium bananas, ripe but still firm, peeled and diced

METHOD

▶ Have someone spoon the ice cream into serving dishes while you are preparing the Banana Salsa, as it cooks quickly.

▶ Melt the butter over low heat in a medium frying pan. Stir in the brown sugar and cinnamon until dissolved. Add the rum, liqueur or orange juice and stir for about 30 seconds. Add the bananas, cook for about 1 minute, until the bananas have softened slightly. Spoon over the ice cream.

139

Salsa Ice Cream

Makes about 1.75 litres/3 pints

If you have an ice-cream maker, you can use the salsas in this chapter in homemade ice cream. If you use Honey-Ginger Peach Salsa, you may want to add 2 more unseeded jalapeños, since the cream muffles their heat.

INGREDIENTS

250 ml/8 fl oz double cream
475 ml/16 fl oz whole milk
2 egg yolks
175 g/6 oz sugar
350 g/12 oz dessert salsa

METHOD

▶ In a medium saucepan, combine the cream and milk and bring to the boil. Remove from the heat and let cool for 10 minutes. In a bowl, beat the egg yolks until they are frothy. Add the sugar and beat for 1 minute. Add a little of the warm milk to the eggs, to raise their temperature gradually without cooking them. Whisk the mixture. Add a little more warm milk, whisking, then gradually mix in the rest of the milk.

▶ Pour the egg-milk mixture into a saucepan and cook over low heat until the custard thickens slightly but does not come to the boil. Remove from the heat, cool, then chill for at least 30 minutes.

▶ Mix the custard with the salsa, then transfer to an ice-cream maker and freeze according to the manufacturer's instructions.

140

Sopapillas

Makes about 20 sopapillas

Sopapillas, little pillows of deep-fried pastry dough, are traditionally served with honey, or sprinkled with cinnamon and sifted icing sugar. For a new twist, try stuffing them with a dessert salsa.

INGREDIENTS

225 g/8 oz plain flour
2 tsp baking powder
½ tsp salt
40 g/1½ oz block margarine
vegetable oil for frying
ground cinnamon
icing sugar
250 g/9 oz dessert salsa of choice

METHOD

▶ Mix the flour, baking powder and salt together in a bowl. Cut the shortening into the flour mixture until it resembles fine crumbs. Add 175 ml/6 fl oz water and knead until it forms a stiff dough, a little moister and more elastic than pastry dough. Wrap in cling film and let rest for about 30 minutes.

▶ On a floured board, roll out half the dough to a thickness of 3 mm/⅛ in. Cut out 7.5-cm/ 3-in squares. Gather up the scraps, combine with the remaining dough, and repeat.

▶ Pour vegetable oil into a deep frying pan to a depth of 2.5–5 cm/1–2 in. Heat to 190°C/ 375°F. The temperature is important because if it is too cold, the sopapillas will be greasy; if it is too hot, the outside of the sopapillas will brown before the inside is cooked. Put a few squares of dough in the hot oil. They should not touch. Cook until puffy and golden brown, turning once, about 1 minute a side. Remove and drain on paper towels. Let the oil return to 190°C/375°F between batches.

▶ Dust the sopapillas with cinnamon and icing sugar. Cut a slit along one edge and stuff with a spoonful of dessert salsa.

141

Cookie Cups with Ricotta Cream and Fruit Salsa

Makes 12 cups, 2 per serving

These desserts are light and elegant. Although the individual components can be made early in the day, the salsa should not be added until just before serving time.

INGREDIENTS FOR COOKIE CUPS

75 g/3 oz toasted pine nuts (see note below)
40 g/1½ oz butter at room temperature
75 g/3 oz sugar
½ tsp vanilla extract
3 egg whites
¼ tsp cinnamon
⅛ tsp salt
5 tbsp plain flour
Ricotta Cream (recipe follows)
*about 175 g/6 oz of dessert fruit salsa of your
    choice*

142

METHOD

▶ Preheat the oven to 190°C/375°F/Gas Mark 5. Grind the roasted pine nuts to crumbs in a food processor, taking care not to let them turn to paste. Set aside.

▶ Line 2 baking sheets with parchment or waxed paper. Have ready an ungreased 12-cup muffin tin.

▶ Cream the butter, sugar and vanilla extract. Add the egg whites, cinnamon and salt, and beat until the mixture is smooth. Add the ground pine nuts and the flour, and mix by hand until smooth once more.

▶ Drop tablespoonfuls of the batter onto the prepared baking sheets, 10 cm/4 in apart. With a rubber spatula, spread the batter into thin, 7.5-cm/3-in circles. Bake until the cookies are firm and have just started to brown around the edges, about 7 minutes. Because you have to work fast with the baked cookies, it is best to bake only one sheet at a time.

▶ As soon as the cookies are done, remove them from the oven. With a wide metal spatula, carefully remove each warm cookie from the sheet, and gently press it into a muffin cup so that it forms a cup. The crimped edges do not need to be uniform. Work quickly so that you get all the cookies into the muffin pan while they are still warm, otherwise, they will crack. Repeat with the second sheet of cookies. Let the cookies cool in the muffin tin. (*Note:* If it is a humid day, the cookies will not get crisp, so leave them in the muffin tin until serving time.)

▶ Divide the Ricotta Cream among the Cookie Cups. This is best done no more than 2 hours before serving time, so that the cookies do not become soggy. Immediately before serving, top each cup with a tablespoon or so of fruit salsa.

INGREDIENTS FOR RICOTTA CREAM

6 tbsp whipping cream
½ tsp vanilla extract
100 g/4 oz ricotta cheese
75 g/3 oz icing sugar

METHOD

▶ Beat the whipping cream with the vanilla extract until soft peaks form. In another bowl, beat together the ricotta cheese and icing sugar. Fold in the whipped cream. Refrigerate until ready to use.

To toast pine nuts: Spread them in a single layer on a baking sheet. Bake at 180°C/350°F/Gas Mark 4 for 5 to 10 minutes until they are golden brown. Watch pine nuts carefully as they burn very quickly.

INDEX

144